Connected Play

The John D. and Catherine T. MacArthur Foundation Series on Digital Media and Learning

Engineering Play: A Cultural History of Children's Software, by Mizuko Ito

Hanging Out, Messing Around, and Geeking Out: Kids Living and Learning with New Media, by Mizuko Ito, Sonja Baumer, Matteo Bittanti, danah boyd, Rachel Cody, Becky Herr-Stephenson, Heather A. Horst, Patricia G. Lange, Dilan Mahendran, Katynka Martínez, C. J. Pascoe, Dan Perkel, Laura Robinson, Christo Sims, Lisa Tripp, with contributions by Judd Antin, Megan Finn, Arthur Law, Annie Manion, Sarai Mitnick, David Schlossberg, and Sarita Yardi

The Civic Web: Young People, the Internet, and Civic Participation, by Shakuntala Banaji and David Buckingham

Connected Play: Tweens in a Virtual World, by Yasmin B. Kafai and Deborah A. Fields

Inaugural Series Volumes

These edited volumes were created through an interactive community review process and published online and in print in December 2007. They are the precursors to the peer-reviewed monographs in the series.

Civic Life Online: Learning How Digital Media Can Engage Youth, edited by W. Lance Bennett

Digital Media, Youth, and Credibility, edited by Miriam J. Metzger and Andrew J. Flanagin

Digital Youth, Innovation, and the Unexpected, edited by Tara McPherson

The Ecology of Games: Connecting Youth, Games, and Learning, edited by Katie Salen

Learning Race and Ethnicity: Youth and Digital Media, edited by Anna Everett

Youth, Identity, and Digital Media, edited by David Buckingham

Connected Play

Tweens in a Virtual World

Yasmin B. Kafai and Deborah A. Fields
foreword by Mizuko Ito

The MIT Press
Cambridge, Massachusetts
London, England

KH

MIT Press books may be purchased at special quantity discounts for business or sales promotional use. For information, please email special_sales@mitpress.mit.edu or write to Special Sales Department, The MIT Press, 55 Hayward Street, Cambridge, MA 02142.

This book was set in Stone Sans and Stone Serif by the MIT Press. Printed and bound in the United States of America.

Library of Congress Cataloging-in-Publication Data

Kafai, Yasmin B.
Connected play : tweens in a virtual world / by Yasmin B. Kafai and Deborah A. Fields.
     pages   cm.—(The John D. and Catherine T. MacArthur Foundation series on digital media and learning)
Includes bibliographical references and index.
ISBN 978-0-262-01993-4 (hardcover : alk. paper)
1. Whyville (Game). 2. Shared virtual environments. 3. Preteens—Recreation. 4. Educational games. I. Fields, Deborah A., author. II. Title.
GV1469.25.W49K34   2013
794.8—dc23
2013013620

10 9 8 7 6 5 4 3 2 1

8/12/15

Contents

Series Foreword

In recent years, digital media and networks have become embedded in our everyday lives and are part of broad-based changes to how we engage in knowledge production, communication, and creative expression. Unlike the early years in the development of computers and computer-based media, digital media are now *commonplace* and *pervasive*, having been taken up by a wide range of individuals and institutions in all walks of life. Digital media have escaped the boundaries of professional and formal practice, and the academic, governmental, and industry homes that initially fostered their development. Now they have been taken up by diverse populations and noninstitutionalized practices, including the peer activities of youth. Although specific forms of technology uptake are highly diverse, a generation is growing up in an era where digital media are part of the taken-for-granted social and cultural fabric of learning, play, and social communication.

This book series is founded upon the working hypothesis that those immersed in new digital tools and networks are engaged in an unprecedented exploration of language, games, social interaction, problem solving, and self-directed activity that leads to diverse forms of learning. These diverse forms of learning are reflected in expressions of identity, how individuals express independence and creativity, and in their ability to learn, exercise judgment, and think systematically.

The defining frame for this series is not a particular theoretical or disciplinary approach, nor is it a fixed set of topics. Rather, the series revolves around a constellation of topics investigated from multiple disciplinary and practical frames. The series as a whole looks at the relation between youth, learning, and digital media, but each might deal with only a subset of this constellation. Erecting strict topical boundaries can exclude some of the most important work in the field. For example, restricting the content of the series only to people of a certain age means artificially reifying an age boundary when the phenomenon demands otherwise. This becomes particularly problematic with new forms of online participation where one important outcome is the mixing of participants of different ages. The same goes for digital media, which are increasingly inseparable from analog and earlier media forms.

The series responds to certain changes in our media ecology that have important implications for learning. Specifically, these are new forms of media *literacy* and changes in the modes of media *participation*. Digital media are part of a convergence between interactive media (most notably gaming), online networks, and existing media forms. Navigating this media ecology involves a palette of literacies that are being defined through practice but require more scholarly scrutiny before they can be fully incorporated pervasively into educational initiatives. Media literacy involves not only ways of understanding, interpreting, and critiquing media, but also the means for creative and social expression, online search and navigation, and a host of new technical skills. The potential gap in literacies and participation skills creates new challenges for educators who struggle to bridge media engagement inside and outside the classroom.

The John D. and Catherine T. MacArthur Foundation Series on Digital Media and Learning, published by the MIT Press, aims to close these gaps and provide innovative ways of thinking about and using new forms of knowledge production, communication, and creative expression.

Foreword

Mizuko Ito

Those of us who study young people and the Internet repeatedly encounter a set of well-meaning concerns voiced by colleagues, parents, and educators. Is online activity good or bad for kids? Does it make them antisocial or violent? Does it disconnect them from their bodies and environments? These concerns, which have been widespread ever since young people started taking up social, mobile, and gaming media, echo earlier concerns over media such as television and radio. As digital and networked technologies make their way into the hands of ever younger children, the need for careful research and balanced perspectives on these issues becomes even more paramount.

This book by Yasmin Kafai and Deborah Fields gently disarms and redirects these concerns toward a productive intergenerational dialogue and positive agenda for educational research and design. The authors do this not by simply asserting their expertise or a moral imperative about children and technology, but through careful observation and representation of the agency, ingenuity, and social conscience of children themselves. The tweens are the stars of the show. Whether through collaboratively grappling with a thorny scientific problem, collectively mobilizing against bad behavior, or developing ingenious "cheats," workarounds, designs, and business models, Whyville is an environment for tweens to exercise agency, problem solving, and social responsibility.

It's not, though, that adults are out of the picture or that this is a world where kids rule. Kafai, Fields, and the educators and technology designers they work with all roll up their sleeves and not only participate in Whyville but work with the tweens to make it a better place. They build new games and educational programs, engage in dialogue, and do research on the way things are, as well as how things might be shaped in the future. This activity demonstrates a mutual respect between kids and adults that is built through shared purpose and interests.

It's this expansive stance toward the future that takes this work well beyond the hand-wringing about new technology and kids that often pervades this field of inquiry. The authors demonstrate how, through active effort, play and learning can be connected across different spheres of life, between the online and the offline, and between people of different ages. It is this kind of meaningful and intentional connectivity that provides our best hope for making the online world a productive force not just for children, but for our collective and increasingly digitally mediated future.

Acknowledgments

This book is the culmination of nearly a decade's worth of research. Yasmin Kafai was fortunate to receive, after several less successful attempts, a grant from the National Science Foundation that jumpstarted the work and resulted in nearly three dozen journal publications and book chapters and more than a hundred presentations at conferences on three continents. Along the way, more than a dozen collaborators joined us for different parts of the analyses and writings. We want to note up front that Numedeon, Inc., the company that owns and hosts Whyville.net, had no control over the publication of the results. None of the authors had any financial interest or any other official relationship with Numedeon—well, except for one time when Yasmin asked for a personal donation of 1,000 clams:

In late 2004 when we were conducting recruitments for the study, Numedeon hosted public sessions in Whyville's Greek Theater to give players a chance to meet us researchers and ask questions. Entering into the Greek Theater, one of the Whyvillians whispered to me, "u r ugly!" I promptly fled the theater and Whyville by closing down the browser. Then I composed myself. This was most likely coming from a twelve-year-old! Truth be told, he or she (in the haste of the moment, I didn't have time to see who had insulted me) was right—my avatar looked nothing special. I had yet to learn about the Whyville way. I went back into the Greek Theater but within the hour I emailed Jen Sun, the president and cofounder of Numedeon. I requested and received a donation of 1,000 clams, the virtual currency in Whyville, so I could better accessorize my avatar. I often tell this story, partly to come clean about my one-time conflict of interest, but mostly to remind myself and others of that visceral reaction and that what happens in virtual worlds is not tangential to players.

We are thankful for Numedeon's willingness—in particular to Jen Sun, Jim Bower, and Mark Dinan—to cooperate in the research studies and to provide access to their logfile data and insights about the workings of Whyville. This is still too rare an event these days. They have graciously read and commented on the papers we have written and continue to remain in conversation with us today, though our views do not necessarily represent theirs.

Most of the work presented here was supported by a grant from the National Science Foundation (NSF-0411814), in addition to a later grant from the MacArthur Foundation to the first author. An Academic Senate grant from the University of California, Los Angeles, provided funding for pilot analyses. The views expressed are those of the authors and do not necessarily represent the views of the National Science Foundation, the John D. and Catherine T. MacArthur Foundation, the University of California, Los Angeles, the University of Pennsylvania, Utah State University, or Numedeon.

Many collaborators have joined us in this long pursuit of understanding tweens' play in Whyville. Cathleen Galas was instrumental in integrating the virtual epidemic WhyPox in science class activities. Brian Foley, now on faculty at CalState Northridge, and Nina Neulight and Linda Kao, then UCLA graduate students, documented classroom and club activities in a pilot study of Whypox. Ron Stevens, a professor of immunology at UCLA School of Medicine, helped us think about the design possibilities of virtual epidemics. Postdoctoral fellow David Feldon helped develop mixed methods early in the study of Whyville that set the stage for much of our later work; he also contributed microanalyses of the simulators of Whypox. Michael Giang has been a long-time contributor to the quantitative analyses presented in chapter 2, in helping us learn to dig through logfiles and in collaborating on mixed methods analyses of tweens' participation. Jason Fields developed innovative ways to use Mathematica for chat data analysis. Then undergraduate researchers Tina Tom and Cameron Aroz helped log massive quantities of video data and assisted in the development of some of the case studies. Kristin Searle developed half of the case studies, those of the boys, reducing clicks and chat to more narrative summaries of daily activity. Melissa Cook contributed much of the analyses concerning race in Whyville, counting the RGB colors of face parts and documenting the inequities reflected in Akbar's and discussed in the *Whyville Times*. Jackie Wong performed analyses on students' argumentation about WhyPox in their sixth grade class. Maria Quintero too delved into students' affectations regarding Whypox infections as part of her master's thesis. Jessica Henderson Costello and Cindy Tran helped document and analyze the 2008 Whyville club, and Cindy Tran especially helped in tracking kids' changes in avatar designs. The research team of Douglas Thomas at the University of Southern California joined us for the study of tweens' flirting and dating online.

Finally, many people in addition to those listed above have provided feedback on our drafts, ideas, and writing along the way. The LTRG research group at UCLA, with Noel Enyedy and William Sandoval, provided invaluable feedback over several years on analyses and writing, bringing us down to earth in our discussions of virtual activities. Special thanks also to William Quinn Burke, Jay Pfaffman, Christon Walker, Jon Wallace, Cliff Zintgraff, and the three anonymous reviewers who provided valuable feedback on earlier and later drafts of book chapters and shaped the directions it has taken. Thanks also to Richard Davis, Veena Vasudevan, and Whitney King for careful reading and copyediting. And of course, thank you to the hundreds of Whyvillians who shared their insights with us and allowed us this glimpse into the virtual lives of tweens. We couldn't have done this without all of you!

1 Playgrounds for Millions

When twelve-year old Zoe (username "bluwave") goes online in the virtual world of Whyville,[1] she checks her bank account for new deposits, shops for clothes for her avatar, tries on new outfits, plays games of checkers, goes to a virtual trading post to exchange clothes, and hangs out with others at the beach. She plays science games to earn some clams, Whyville's virtual currency. She chats with friends from school and meets new people. She flirts a little. She even tries to cheat people out of their clams for a couple of weeks. Her interest in these activities will change over time; some will grow tiresome to her, while others will become more engrossing, occupying more of her time online.

At first sight, Zoe's play in Whyville doesn't seem much different from that of other kids playing offline. She's playing with her looks and judging how people respond to her; she's flirting; she's learning to earn and manage money; she's playing games and also scamming. As others have observed, virtual worlds include many mundane activities that are normal for kids playing with other kids.[2] Familiar issues like understanding oneself, learning how to respond to other people, and developing a code of ethics are at the heart of growing up.

At second glance, some aspects of Zoe's play seem quite distinct from offline play. Players can do things digitally that are difficult (or awkward) to do physically: throw smiley faces at friends, simulate rocket launches, or change clothes in an instant. And not only clothes—players can also change their skin color, hair, lips, eyes, ears, and noses. They can actually be anything that can be drawn. Past Whyvillians have been soda cans, carrots, pharaohs, pixies, even Barack Obama. Kids also hang out with thousands, if not millions, of other kids, not just with those in the playgrounds and schoolyards of their neighborhoods.

Play in these virtual worlds is both similar to and different from what we know about the way kids have played in the past. This book is about reimagining kids' play in the new digital publics[3]—the virtual backyards, street corners, schoolyards, and shopping malls that have become playgrounds for millions of kids in the twenty-first century. With names like Habbo Hotel, Toontown, and Whyville, these virtual worlds suggest buildings of brick and mortar and cities with homes, streets, and neighborhoods, but in the digital domain. Millions of kids visit these virtual worlds every day. In particular, tweens, kids aged nine to twelve, are at a critical age as they transition from childhood into adolescence and their teens. As adults have put increased limits on outdoor and even indoor spaces, virtual worlds and gaming sites have figured much more prominently as centers for play. Revealing the opportunities, challenges, and dynamics of these digital playgrounds is one of the main goals of this book.[4]

We chose to call the book *Connected Play* because of the fundamental ways that digital publics extend play from the everyday spaces of kids' lives at home, in school, in clubs, and with friends, and because of the social connections created and sustained through such play that are among its primary values for friendship, family relations, and new online acquaintances. Connections are at the core of play in the digital playgrounds of the twenty-first century. We intend to illuminate what happens when kids play in virtual worlds, how this matters for their lives beyond those digital playgrounds, and what educational opportunities can be found or designed in and with those worlds.

The Digital Side of Play

We want to reimagine kids' play, to transform what we think of play and what it can be in the twenty-first century. To do this we must first understand what is familiar about kids' play in virtual worlds, what is uniquely different, and how the familiar and the different intertwine. As we will share throughout this book, many priorities from kids' everyday lives extend into the digital domain. Virtual worlds provide open but designed spaces where kids can freely socialize with peers in imaginative and fun ways; many kids extend relationships with existing friends by logging in and playing from their homes. Instead of calling one another on the phone, they play together online. Not only friendships, but also interests, values, and issues of growing up are significant in kids' play in virtual worlds, extending from home, school, friendships, and hobbies. Yet there are also unique opportunities (or challenges, as the case may be) for kids playing in a digital playground rather than a physical one. What are the distinct dimensions of play in *digital* publics, and how do they connect to kids' social, ethical, and creative development?

The first and most obvious distinction is the huge size of this new digital playground. Kids meet and interact with hundreds, thousands, potentially millions of other kids.[5] This teeming, populous digital public is unprecedented. Kids have always connected with different groups and communities, but virtual communities cross boundaries in ways that were not previously possible. What kinds of relationships develop when there are so many kids together in a digital space? What do kids reveal about themselves as they navigate relationships? What role does anonymity play, especially when kids are told not to divulge personally identifying information about themselves? Digital spaces are unique not only because of the sheer number of kids who socialize within them, but also because of the ways in which their socializing is mediated.

Virtual spaces have many features that shape how kids communicate and interact with each other, forming a second unique dimension of digital publics. Digital mechanics trace social connections and activities as kids interact, leaving "networking residue"[6] through friend lists, gifts sent, messages left on profiles, even the ability to "silence" offensive others or make them invisible. Chat can be broadcast widely to large groups of people in a virtual room or whispered privately to an individual. Likewise, kid-designed digital objects, such as drawn avatar parts and written articles published in virtual worlds, raise interesting issues of ownership and copyright. Players might not be aware that their networking residues and contributions in the form of interactions, clicks, chat, messages, and designs are recorded by companies and searched, collated, and analyzed by those with access. This brings up issues of privacy, copyright, ethics, and quality of play.[7]

A third distinction is that play in the digital public affords unusual design opportunities for kids: ways to customize their appearances, "homes," and digital products in flexible ways not as easily available in the physical domain. Using digital paint and assembly tools, kids can create highly diverse types of avatars—online characters—and look like almost anyone or anything they want. They also have opportunities to create and customize their own houses and online "bedrooms" with few of the physical limitations and costs of such construction. What kids make for themselves can often be produced and sold to millions of their peers, creating a massive audience for digital products. Although these design opportunities suggest an idealized space for a "second life" without prejudices or constraints, the claims that have portrayed the Internet as a sort of utopian realm have proven to be less than realistic. What kinds of design opportunities do virtual worlds offer, how do kids use them, and to what effect? Social pressures, design constraints, and difficulties with learning design tools all influence the degree to which kids take advantage of and learn to use design opportunities online. Further, despite a potential audience of millions, it can be difficult to draw attention to one's creations.

Finally, a fourth unique dimension of digital publics is that they are designed spaces that are open to change. Perhaps more than other spaces we occupy, every object, surface, and even the mechanisms for talking, chatting, and looking certain ways were created. This means they can also be changed. These spaces and their interfaces are managed in many ways, from chat filters down to legal end-user agreements.[8] All of the special affordances of networking, design opportunities, and a massive public in virtual communities are designed in regard to the freedom and constraints they give to players to realize these opportunities. In other words, many but not all of Zoe's (bluwave) interactions and choices are preconfigured in both visible and less visible ways. Yet she and other players also use these designed worlds in ways both intended and unintended by their designers. Various cultural forces shape how designers design and how kids play with and within these designs. This last point merits particular attention because the design of virtual play spaces will influence kids' opportunities for learning and personal growth in significant ways.

Play in digital publics has the potential to provide new forms to engage with others and creatively design for others, offering opportunities for social development, creative expression, and learning. Yet it is unclear whether and how this kind of play lives up to its potential. We need to understand how kids are engaging with others, to what degree what they are doing is new and different, and what new and/or familiar challenges they face. And we need to understand what it takes to get the most out of play in virtual worlds, and who is doing so. Then we can think more carefully about design features and situations of play that allow kids greater opportunities for growing up. Like the slides and swings on neighborhood playgrounds, we want features and spaces to be safe for kids while leaving enough freedom for responsible play to provide engaging opportunities and challenges for learning. To address these competing demands, we need to look at virtual worlds from multiple connected perspectives that encompass considerations from developmental and cultural researchers as well as those from digital media scholars and learning technologists.

The Serious Side of Play

Play is fundamentally important for kids' development. The principal role of play spaces such as sidewalks, parks, and playgrounds, as well as activities with toys and games, is to promote social interactions between kids.[9] We know that when they play with peers, kids are free to experiment with rules and design their own pretend scenarios or practices that set the stage for creativity and empathy. Power, recognition, fairness, sharing, morality, and friendship are all negotiated among peers at play. Furthermore, play is not cut off from everyday life, but rather extends from kids' experiences in home, school, and other social environments. Kids take values and rules from those spaces and "play" with them: trying out new scenarios, testing values, establishing morals, and coming up with creative new ideas.[10] Indeed, many researchers have argued that children figure out social roles and learn to negotiate with each other as they navigate and define the rules of games. Put simply, peer play helps kids develop socially, cognitively, and culturally. To cut children off from peer play is to cut them off from one of the most essential forms of learning and innovating. So what do we need to understand and promote about playfulness among kids in digital publics?

To answer this question, we need to adopt a new perspective on play, one that values not only its developmental and cultural contributions but also its connections to learning and literacy in the opportunities for creative design and intentional reflection it offers in these digital arenas of play. We see play as a voluntary activity that kids engage in for pursuing their interests, experimenting with boundaries, and expressing themselves. We define play as interacting both within and outside the boundaries of these designed spaces. Thus, play is about conforming and experimenting with norms and values that have been designed into digital publics and those that are designed and put forward by players. Our definition of play includes games of construction that psychologist Jean Piaget[11] saw as an essential but often forgotten part of development. We see play as a stepping stone for kids to develop important competencies that include social and design practices that they engage in across cultures. We argue that if one wants to understand and design play spaces in the digital public, one must first understand play. Such an integrative approach values the different contributions that various perspectives provide on play: understanding the individual player and developmental needs, understanding that players are shaped by cultural norms and practices, and understanding the designed and participatory nature of digital media.

Nowhere is this importance of various perspectives more apparent than in digital publics, which are constructed environments that embody ideas about players and their competencies but are also constructed through the interactions and contributions of players themselves. From a developmental perspective, we understand that play provides opportunities and challenges for kids to learn how to navigate new situations. From a cultural perspective, we understand that play is about learning the norms and values of a culture. From a media perspective, we understand that participation is not just about critical understanding but also about learning technical skills that support participation and contribution. One could argue that these playgrounds for millions are cultures of their own, distinguishable from their physical counterparts, but this would draw a distinction based purely on technical grounds. Rather, it is appropriate to understand children's play in the digital public as play that is occurring in a different context that might well have connections with their play in the physical realm.

Thus, to understand and promote play in the digital public means leaving behind academic boundaries artificially drawn around the study of play that focus either on developmental benefits, critical understandings, or technical skills alone.[12] Rather, it is about developing a more connected view of what anthropologist Marjorie Goodwin called "the serious side" of play when she studied jumping rope on playgrounds for its larger cultural relevance.[13] The play we observed and studied in virtual worlds is not separate from kids' everyday lives; rather, it is an integral activity that exists across digital platforms regardless of where and how we study it. We can easily extend Goodwin's argument that "children may in fact discover how social order works through game participation"[14] from jumping rope to avatars engaging with others in the virtual activities such as teleporting and throwing mudballs. Like jumping rope, play in digital publics requires knowing how to *play* in a new domain, how to *play well* with others, and how to *play creatively*. To gain the benefits of play in massive digital playgrounds, kids need to know how to use digital tools and spaces, how to socialize with vast numbers of kids in conditions of relative anonymity that bring moral issues to the fore, and how to create with and push back against the designs of these settings. Below we elaborate on each of these ideas in turn.

Learning how to *play* in digital playgrounds is not as easy as it looks. To those unfamiliar with virtual worlds, it may seem as though everyone knows what to do and where to go. But a closer look reveals that participation in these sites is not equal—kids participate to differing degrees and in a variety of ways. Certainly we know that players exhibit stark differences: some play a lot and others hardly at all. What is less clear is the quality of their play. We also know that participation in virtual worlds does not seem to come naturally—at least not to everyone—and that players have to develop the competencies to marshal multiple resources across settings. Developing these competencies can mean various things, ranging from designing an avatar to look socially acceptable to knowing where to go to find others to play with. Sometimes it even involves learning new words, terms, and phrases to understand what others are saying. How kids learn to navigate digital publics is largely invisible. Many detailed ethnographies and reports describe the complexities of how adolescent and adult players learn to become members of massive online gaming communities, but it's really not clear how younger people navigate their equally complex virtual worlds.[15] Thus, one of our goals is to illuminate how kids learn to be insiders in these digital playgrounds.

Using digital tools—and using them in culturally relevant ways—is vital to connected play in digital playgrounds. Participating involves a technical understanding of how to navigate interfaces, manipulate tools, and share content, as well as a cultural understanding of knowing how to do so appropriately. For example, learning how to make an avatar involves not only using tools for layering eyes, nose, lips, hair, and clothing, but also making the avatar look good to others. How many times did Whyvillians tell us that we looked ugly, even after we had spent hours working on our avatars' looks! Thus, although using technology effectively has often been portrayed as a simple issue of access to computers and the Internet, Henry Jenkins more accurately describes these access issues as a "participation gap."[16] Learning the skills to become a full member of a digitally based community can be challenging, and there are different kinds and levels of membership. Kids need a variety of technical skills to become digitally literate or fluent, but often adults focus on the technical over the important cultural and social forms of participation required for full membership in online communities. This idea captures the full spectrum of what Mizuko Ito and colleagues have described as "hanging out, messing around, and geeking out."[17] Learning a range of participation practices—from socializing to manipulating digital tools to one's own ends—is important for kids who are learning to play connectively in virtual worlds, providing important stepping stones into other digital publics.

Learning how to *play well* is another layer of connected play in virtual worlds. Beyond the technical or cultural ins and outs, it's also important to know how to engage and socialize with others in a responsible manner in these massive, often anonymous environments.[18] Virtual worlds, social network sites, and massively multiplayer games contain huge potential to support social and ethical learning. Where there are opportunities to interact with many different people, it's easy to treat others poorly because we don't know them, because they have no power over us, or because we will never see them again. In digital as well as other playgrounds, kids try out different actions and often hurt each other in the process. Yet not only in virtual spaces but in many areas of everyday life, our actions influence people whom we do not know. Can virtual worlds offer an opportunity to engage kids in learning to treat others with respect and stepping into others' shoes?

A related issue concerns responsible play. We want play spaces to be safe places for kids to venture into and learn new things or simply have fun. Adults aren't always around to monitor play. In fact, one important lesson of growing up means knowing what to do when someone is being physically or verbally abused.[19] Many sites have various safeguards in place to prevent or respond to these kinds of issues: chat filters, chat selection menus, community monitors, emergency messaging tools. How do kids respond to different safeguards? How much can kids manage themselves and where do we need to provide support? How can we help kids connect values and morals from home, school, and communities to their interactions in virtual worlds? Answering these questions requires an in-depth understanding of the performance of play in digital publics and how kids actually respond to safeguards, scenarios, and ethical dilemmas—information we provide in this book, which should inform the designs of digital playgrounds and guide those who work with the kids who play in them. This information is also of concern to the kids themselves, as we found out in our discussions with Whyvillians.

Finally, learning how to *play creatively* touches on design and agency in digital playgrounds. A significant aspect of creative play is captured in players' developing or designing content. In the context of virtual worlds, this might include giving players freedom to customize their avatars to reflect their real and imagined desires. Or a site might provide design tools that let players create and share their own avatar parts or design other objects such as houses, airplanes, cars, or even mini-games. Thus players have the ability to create content, allowing them to produce things that become a part of these digital playgrounds. Of course, thinking about what kids can create in virtual worlds means attending to the design tools and infrastructures for sharing content that shape what kids can make and how they can share things. Who is allowed to design things, and what do they design? How do the design tools and infrastructures shape what can be and what is created? How does the community respond to these designs? How creative are the designs themselves? One reason to attend to creative designs in virtual worlds is that these designed objects can be sites for witnessing connections between kids' desires, values, experiences, and their designed objects. What do kids choose to embody in their creative designs in virtual worlds, and what does this tell us about the connectedness of their play?

Another aspect of playing creatively concerns the level of agency allowed to kids in a digital public. One level of agency is how much freedom kids get to represent themselves online, for instance from choosing between preset characters to creating their own images. Yet we also need to consider agency in the context of understanding the design of the virtual community at large, for the simple reason that designs can make room for creative and expressive play. If one important aspect of play is trying out new rules, roles, and ideas, then how much does the design of a given world let kids do so? Game researcher Sebastian Deterding suggests that one important aspect of playfulness is benign transgression: playing with the rules and infringing on them, though not maliciously.[20] How much does the design of a given world let kids try out new rules, roles, and ideas? What forms of agency do kids exhibit, and how do these forms of agency help kids play with the designs and intentions of the virtual world?

Considering the design of a virtual world writ large also brings up what digital media researchers refer to as transparency. Transparency means making visible how online worlds are created, recognizing who has vested interests in them (i.e., who owns them or how they earn money), and understanding how and by whom messages are shaped. Here designers can think about providing access to data and tools that players could manipulate to gain further insights into their virtual play. How much insight do designers give into the inner workings of the virtual world? What does it mean when kids themselves have some role in the design of various elements of the virtual world? Do players take advantage of such creative opportunities, and if so, how? In what ways do these creative opportunities alleviate or reproduce social inequities online? In other words, we consider agency to be an issue not just of understanding and representing oneself online but also of understanding others and the world around us.

Many stakeholders, not just the players themselves, are concerned with the questions and issues presented here. Parents, educators, researchers, policy makers, and designers all have a growing interest in the opportunities that virtual worlds provide for kids. Businesses, certainly, have taken notice of virtual worlds as a growing market, and they are developing online worlds specifically targeted at children, often rife with advertisements and connecting toy purchases with play in virtual worlds. Educators and researchers are developing virtual worlds for kids with educational goals in mind, hoping to take advantage of the ability to design simulations and scenarios for understanding scientific ideas and to put design tools into the hands of kids themselves. Parents and teachers may wonder about these strange worlds and what opportunities or pitfalls they hold for their kids. Yet relatively little has been published on how kids play in these digital playgrounds. Commercial developers carefully protect their information on who is playing and how. Virtual worlds developed by nonprofits and educational researchers are small and few in number compared to their commercial counterparts. They are also often much more structured, meant to be used in conjunction with a school curriculum rather than as a space for free play. So how can we learn about kids' connected play in virtual worlds? Here we come to our investigation of a long-standing virtual world, Whyville (http://whyville. net). Whyville offered us the opportunity to be both observers and designers in a massive online world frequented by tweens.

Why Whyville?

Whyville now counts more than 5.6 million members and 40 million monthly page views.[21] It bills itself as an informal science site where members can register for free, play science games to accrue virtual currency called clams that they can spend to accessorize their online representations (i.e., avatars), and socialize with others. We've already told you a little about Zoe and some of her everyday activities in Whyville, but that was only a sampling of the many things tweens do there.

Whyville contains dozens of science games, some of them collaborative, that Whyvillians can play to earn clams. Leveling up in games boosts the daily salary that players get when they log in each day. Bank accounts store information on daily income, purchases, certificates of deposit, and interest. Players spend many of their clams in a virtual shopping mall called Akbar's, which has over 30,000 avatar accessorizing parts ("face parts") of hair, lips, eyes, and clothes for any occasion—all designed by Whyvillians. In fact, regularly shopping for and accessorizing their avatars is among Whyvillians' favorite activities. Designing and selling face parts provides yet another form of income where players can own stores, advertise their goods, and evaluate production costs. The virtual trading posts allow for exchanges of face parts and the occasional scam. There are over a hundred different places to visit. Some are public and popular, like the City Beach where Whyvillians hang out and socialize; others, such as the Moon, are accessible only to those who know secret teleporting commands. Whyvillians read and contribute to an online newspaper, the *Whyville Times*, which has archived more than 10,000 newspaper articles published over thirteen years. Whyvillians can participate in elections, beauty pageants, proms, and other events, some designed by Numedeon, the company that hosts and owns Whyville, and many created by Whyvillians.

In our study of this virtual world, we eventually became Whyvillians ourselves, simply as a result of spending hundreds of hours there: accumulating clams, mastering science games, trying out different looks, even getting a loan for our first online car. We often marveled at what we observed, and for a time kept a blog called *Everything Whyville* to record and share our observations. We found out later that we were not the only ones to do so. Hundreds of Whyvillians also keep a public presence outside of Whyville, sharing their insights of online life on cheat sites, which often include shortcuts to science games or tips on navigating the site, activities we discuss in more detail in chapter 5.

We had several reasons to choose Whyville to understand connected play. The first, as we've already noted, is its massive scale—its more than 5.6 million registered players make it comparable to larger commercial virtual worlds. To put Whyville's size into perspective, Habbo Hotel, the leader among virtual worlds (albeit for teens) counts more than 268 million registered members, with over 9 million unique users every month.[22] Though more recent data are difficult to obtain, in 2009 sites directed toward children aged 6 to 14 advertised populations of 28 million (Club Penguin), 54 million (Neopets, with 128,000 monthly visitors), and 75 million (Poptropica).[23] All of these virtual worlds are owned by big media corporations such as Sulake (Habbo Hotel), Disney (Club Penguin and Toontown), and Viacom (Neopets). Though Whyville is much smaller than these corporate-owned virtual worlds, Whyvillians spend an average of three hours per month for a total of 5 million hours on the site. These demographics make Whyville one of the "stickiest" virtual worlds online, even when compared to its commercial cousins.[24]

A second reason is the makeup of Whyville's player population, which counts players aged 8 to 18 years (plus some older players), with an average age of 12.3 years. This is an interesting and diverse age group in which players are fairly literate and still engaged in play, but with a growing interest in romantic relationships. It is a time when peers become a more important reference group. Kids at the early to mid-point of this age group, the tweens, sit between childhood and adolescence. As with any transitional stage, it is a short but intense life period with many challenges; much of what tweens do is aspirational, as they look forward to becoming more independent. Further, two-thirds of Whyville's players are girls. In 2002, when we started our research in Whyville, this was a unique feature; at the time, many people presumed that most girls were not interested in computers. Today, the differences in computer and Internet use between girls and boys have nearly disappeared, with the exception of video game play. Whyville was an early example of this trend. Moreover, although tween girls often opt out of science, they chose to frequent Whyville even though it billed itself explicitly as an informal science site.

A third reason is that Whyville is both a popular, free-time-based virtual world and a site with an explicit focus on education, particularly science learning. Whyville started in 1999 as an outreach effort by Jim Bower, then a professor of neuroscience at the California Institute of Technology, and Jen Sun, who holds a PhD in neuroscience and served as CEO of Numedeon. Science games and experiences form some of the core activities in Whyville. One such science experience is an innovative type of community game simulating a virtual epidemic that infects the community and gives players first-hand experience with studying an infectious disease outbreak. Combining science and free play experiences makes Whyville an unusual and interesting site, illustrating what relatively unstructured play in digital publics looks like and how it could be designed to engage players educationally. It also allowed us to design and observe our very own virtual epidemic—more about this in chapter 6.

Finally, the hosts of Whyville consented to collecting data and tracking players for extended periods of time (with players' and their parents' signed permission). This was uniquely important for understanding connected play. Though there are several excellent examples of careful ethnographies by researchers who spent extensive time in virtual worlds such as Second Life, EverQuest, and World of Warcraft, as well as studies that have analyzed substantial logfile data sets or surveys from thousands of players, these two modes of analysis have rarely been combined.[25] So far, researchers have not been able to connect careful observations online with the actual movements of players on a large scale. Whyville allowed us to do this by giving us access to the logfile data of hundreds of consenting players, a subset of whom we could directly observe in classes and an after-school club and indirectly observe when they logged on from their homes. Such a treasure trove of data let us get at some of the networking residue that is often hidden or not made accessible to researchers. Whyville thus provided a unique but promising case study of play in a digital public because we could connect the dots both online and offline, between players together in person and together (or alone) online in a massive community, and between activities in class and online discussions.

Our work took place over several years, with a preliminary study in 2002 and a very extensive study in 2005, followed by shorter interventions and observations in 2008 and 2009. Conducting research in a virtual world, especially one populated by minors, posed many interesting ethical and methodological challenges.[26] Most obvious were the significant age differences between the players and the researchers, which might also explain why up to now most of the researched virtual worlds and gaming communities have been those populated by adults—players of roughly the same age as the researchers. Anyone can join Whyville and participate after a three-day waiting period—a feature set up by the company to discourage lurking.[27] In addition, we ourselves engaged in hundreds of hours of play online, becoming Whyvillians, though we were identifiable as researchers by our special Whyologist hats. Thus the first-person accounts so prominent in current research about online communities also informed our perspective and understanding as to what happened in Whyville.

We spent time on the site getting to know places, playing games, and working hard to create promising avatar appearances. Nonetheless, we stood out, and not just because of our Whyologist hats. Our avatar looks and chat lingo were clearly different from those of other players on the site. We had trouble completely fitting in with the trends of language and looks among tweens in Whyville. When directly approached, we explained why we were there. There were also public sessions in which we introduced research to recruit participants. In general, Whyvillians felt positive about our presence, though on occasion some would comment on our "ugly" appearance (see the acknowledgments). Many of them thought that our research would help Whyville become a better place, and they saw their participation in surveys as a form of community service; some even asked to join our research team. In a few instances, such as when visiting trading rooms, we were shushed when players felt we had interrupted what they considered to be private interactions. Yet there is no denying that for us, being in Whyville was like being in a different world, whereas our club participants seemed to join the virtual community more seamlessly after an initial period of exploration.

Though our presence was not hidden, some of our research was not directly visible to Whyville players. Most notably, the logfile collection continued silently over six months (though players and their parents had been informed and had given their signed consent). Given the long time frame, three months in the club and six months online, it is easy to understand that players would simply forget after a while that every mouse click and chat line was being recorded,[28] potentially analyzed, and linked with other sources. The logfiles were recorded twenty-four hours a day, seven days a week, from January to June 2005. We thus captured play on evenings and weekends in addition to the school-day play simultaneously observed in the classes and the after-school club. We saw instances of inappropriate chat and scamming[29] that otherwise might not have been visible to us (see chapters 4 and 5). And we know from the debriefing interviews that we conducted with club players that they chose not to mention their often extensive flirting and cheating, perhaps because they didn't consider it socially desirable, even though these were widespread activities among Whyvillians.

We also connect online and offline play, and intentionally so, because transitions were often seamless. How often did we watch a dozen tweens in the club logging in to Whyville and shouting out to each other across the room when their avatars met on the screen or teleported together to the Moon for mudball slinging! By the same token, we equally often observed instances when club members would not recognize each other online and say to each other with a puzzled look on their faces, "That's you?!" Through our observations, online and in the club, we were able to generate more connected accounts of play as we followed players or, sometimes, particular practices such as learning the secret command of teleporting. Have you ever wondered how players find out about such secret commands? Insights such as these, small in nature but large in impact, capture and connect play and learning in the digital public.

Book Overview

In this book, we provide a detailed portrait of connected play in the virtual world of Whyville that touches on the universal themes of knowing how to play, and doing so well and responsibly, with others in the digital public. Several audiences have a growing interest in understanding the opportunities and challenges associated with connected play. Educational and developmental psychologists will be interested in the dynamics of tweens' play in virtual worlds and how issues like identity, social development, romantic relationships, gender, and ethics are woven into their activities. Parents and educators will attend to the opportunities for learning that can be built into these worlds and how best to shape and scaffold these opportunities through interactive play in clubs, classrooms, and home environments. Digital media scholars will appreciate our attention to young adolescents, or tweens, a population generally left out of most literature on young people's use of digital media. They will also be interested in the multimodal methods we've developed to study kids in digital sites of play as well as the practices of creative design that kids use in virtual worlds. Finally, developers of online social media will learn about some of the ways to take advantage of kids' abilities and interests in large-scale digital environments, with implications for designing such environments for "stickiness" and interest.

Chapter 2 takes us deep into the heart of Whyville to reveal the inner lives of tween players. We follow the digital footprints of tweens in Whyville, drawing on our unique access to track the movements and interactions of over 500 tweens for a period of six months, coupled with observations captured in video records, field notes, and interviews with some of the players in after-school clubs and science classes. We begin by describing a typical day in a virtual world. This simple step is important because much of what we know and hear about virtual worlds focuses on a few highlighted and sometimes problematic incidents that fail to capture the larger range of activities in which tweens actually engage. We then proceed to recount one girl's changing patterns of participation in Whyville and how those matched larger trends on the site (and, by extension, in other virtual worlds) as well as how they connected to other areas of her everyday life. We end with descriptions of play that crossed the boundaries of Whyville and school friendships from an after-school club. Such access to the intimate details of online life is rare, and it gives us multiple perspectives on Whyville, from the broad trends of hundreds of players, across social interactions between friends in a computer club, and within one player's developing life.

Chapter 3 examines identity play in the context of avatar design and how issues of race, gender, and personal expression become apparent through designs and discussions as tweens create their online representations. Few topics about being online have received more attention than developing an online persona, as this has often been portrayed as an opportunity to be anyone one wants, to have a "second life." Yet in Whyville, how kids choose to look is an intricate decision based on self-reflection, the choices available to them, and social pressures. Design choices provoke conversations about gender, race, disguise, and personal tastes. They reveal social pressures and cultures in Whyville. One subsection in this chapter, "Blacks Deserve Bodies Too," introduces how kids in Whyville dealt with inequities of representation in their avatars, especially when they were the ones producing (and reproducing) racial disparities in avatar parts. Designing avatars brings to the fore issues about what tools and parts are available to represent oneself and how tweens represent themselves over time.

In chapter 4, we take a closer look at the social play that drives most of the interactions among tweens in virtual worlds, whether they're hanging out on the virtual beach or teleporting together to the depths of the solar system. This chapter is very much about the social connections that played out between kids in Whyville, across school, home, and other spaces, between friends and strangers, and with the opposite sex. We draw on surveys from hundreds of Whyville players who talk about their experiences friending others online, in addition to our observations from logfiles and in-person club interactions. The section entitled "Valentine Games" is a unique introduction to the world of flirting and dating in Whyville and how tweens experiment with romantic relationships. Much of this flirting is anticipatory and not fully realized—who, after all, can call dozens of other players "girlfriend" or "boyfriend" after just a few chats? Nonetheless, anticipatory flirting is a frequent part of new activities seen as an essential aspect of growing up. We know that for tweens in particular this is a sensitive and awkward time where clear lines are drawn between boys and girls playing together or apart. If it's true that social networking technologies, including virtual worlds like Whyville and Second Life, are becoming the architects of our intimate relationships, then paying attention to how tweens relate to one another in a virtual world can help us design places where social play and experimentation are safe and open.

In chapter 5 we turn to kids' playful testing of ethical boundaries in virtual worlds. In particular we consider "boundary play" in the broad context of cheating, a practice often condemned in society but commonly accepted and even recommended in gaming. On one level, cheating takes kids beyond the actual boundaries of virtual worlds on hundreds of sites maintained by kids to construct and share cheats, that is, shortcuts to science games and tips on insider knowledge of virtual cultures. A surprising but insightful upside of this type of cheating is that it informs designs of good educational games: games that require only simple cheats do not provide rich opportunities for learning, whereas those that involve complex cheats move beyond just memorizing facts and require cheaters and players alike to engage in deeper, often collaborative inquiry. A broader view of cheating raises ethical issues ranging from relatively benign transgressions of designers' intentions to outright scams of other kids. In our subsection entitled "Stealing from Grandma," we share Whyvillians' open discussions of this central part of digital life in the *Whyville Times*, as they debate the ethics of cheating games, cheating players, cheating in elections, and cheating on virtual boyfriends. Against this backdrop, we discuss the short-lived scams of two of the more intense players from the after-school club. Playing with boundaries raises provocative discussions of ethics and learning and provides a fruitful context to consider how to engage kids in learning to play thoughtfully and creatively.

Understanding connected play is an essential precursor to understanding designs for learning in virtual worlds. In chapter 6, we study the design and outbreak of WhyPox, a virtual epidemic, as a context for learning about infectious disease in clubs and classrooms. With the disappearance of many childhood infections, few children have direct experiences with epidemic outbreaks other than reading or hearing about smallpox epidemics in the past or bird flu outbreaks in Asia today. However, simulating epidemics in virtual worlds can give kids effective and instructional experiences for understanding infectious disease, engaging them in complex problem solving and collaborative interactions as they investigate the causes of the epidemic. Virtual epidemics, a type of what we call community games, draw together principles of effective games while also engaging whole communities of kids in the experience safely. They can also easily link to broader classroom investigations of infectious disease, allowing them to connect experiences and investigations in the virtual world with science learning in classes or clubs.

In chapter 7, we examine design opportunities for play and learning in virtual worlds. While toys and playgrounds have a long history of being designed for entertainment, education, and children's safety, players themselves often design virtual worlds, especially their content. What does it mean to design opportunities for play and learning? We review the opportunities for creative and expressive play in virtual worlds, realizing that the level of avatar-customization features in Whyville is unique compared to the canned features in many commercial virtual worlds. Next, a case study of how a collective of Whyville players worked on developing a cheat to a new science game provides a compelling illustration of how cheating can be good for learning. Finally, we consider how to design for connections across spaces like clubs, classrooms, and other virtual sites and how to support constructive play that emphasizes the creative potential of youth.

In the final chapter, we turn to the future of play and draw conclusions from what we have learned about connected play in virtual worlds. These lessons have ramifications for how we think about the design of digital experiences in other types of virtual communities for kids. Relatively simple changes illustrate how, even in Whyville, we could design for greater levels of agency for players to enrich their engagement and learning. In particular, we discuss virtual worlds that are more design oriented, where kids are given tools to contribute original content that requires multiple levels of technical and social competence. Chapter notes are included at the end of the book for those interested in following up with further readings; in particular several of our papers that examine the topics discussed in the book provide greater detail. Research notes provide a more detailed account of how participants were recruited and how the data were collected and analyzed.

2 Digital Footprints

When I first joined Whyville, I dressed my face the way I liked it. "Realistic" proportions. It looked good to me! I started exploring, and soon found out all the action happened in South Beach. So I went, thinking, 'I hope I'll fit in.' But, I was shunned my first day. Someone just came up to me when I was minding my own business. By nature, my first approach was a friendly, "Hi! What's up?" Guess what the reply was? "Wow! You're ugly!"

That was the last of me. I clicked that life saver red x. I'm done, that's all I thought. I don't want anything to do with Whyville. I was wrong. I found myself in front of the computer two days later. The address bar read: www.whyville.com. I took a deep breath, pressed enter, and focused. I tried again.—click—clear—Goodbye, "ugly."

I practiced. I made a new face. I cleared it. New face, clear. I watched videos, I visited the Style Salon everyday, for a month. The videos helped most. I had all the parts, I put them up right. Everything in Whyville proportion. No matter how many clams I spent on parts, how much I scoured the pages of Akbar's Face Mall, it didn't feel right. It wasn't "like them."

—ElEmAyeOh[1]

What do we know about kids' play in virtual worlds? The truth is that we really don't know much. This is particularly true for tweens, since most research has focused on either teens or young adults.[2] Further, few details in the reports that do discuss tweens go very deep into what they actually do online.[3] While these reports generally mention the frequency of tweens' game play, they do not differentiate between different kinds of games or ask about what kinds of social activities kids may be engaging in through their game play.

So, what do we know? We know that it is important for kids to have a few close friends as well as a number of friendly acquaintances—essentially a healthy mix of strong ties and weak ties in terms of relationships. Some researchers suggest that social network sites for teens and young adults can provide supportive spaces to develop these weak ties in nonthreatening ways. We also know that it is important for kids to learn how to express themselves both in terms of who they are and who they would like to be across a variety of settings. And we know that kids learn and adapt the social rules of society through their play with each other.[4]

In this chapter, we look over tweens' shoulders as they play on Whyville. We begin by following up with Zoe, whom we introduced in chapter 1, sharing typical activities in her first weeks. Then we consider other members of the after-school club of which she was a part, demonstrating the resourceful ways that she and other members of the club learned insider practices on Whyville by describing how they took up teleporting, followed by more details on Zoe's Whyville life: her growing specializations in trade, her exploration in creating an online identity, and some of her more scandalous (if temporary) scamming. Zoe is one of six case studies that we developed from members of the club, each of whom shared some common practices with the others while also establishing his or her own personal trajectories in Whyville. At the end of the chapter we cast a wider net by reviewing broad trends in play and players on Whyville community at large.

A Typical Day in Whyville

One of the questions we began with was how tweens adapted to a new virtual setting. Given our own awkwardness in figuring out how to talk, look, and just "be" in Whyville, how did tweens learn to navigate Whyville? This appears to be no trivial matter, as EIEmAyeOh's account at the beginning of this chapter reveals. We turned primarily to members of the after-school club because all of the members were new to Whyville. We closely studied the activities of their first few weeks in Whyville and noticed that most began with similar patterns before branching out in ways that were more personal and unique.

Consider Zoe,[5] a twelve-year-old, sixth-grade, African-American girl from our after-school club and class whom we introduced in chapter 1. Zoe was an early "Whyville expert" in the club from whom other members sought help with games and trading parts for avatars. When she joined Whyville, her first step was to pick a name for her avatar (a virtual representation that looks like a two-dimensional cartoon character). She chose a username that had symbolic meaning to her: "I first wanted 'angel,' they were all gone, even with all the numbers," she explained. So instead Zoe chose a name that sparkled "so I can shine."[6] We chose "bluwave" as a pseudonym[7] to mirror her choice of username. Other club members also chose usernames that reflected something about them—a love of animals (whskr29), an interest in games (xboxman, raybeams), wordplays on favorite characters from movies (wiseyoda, vulcan61), favorite shoes (uggs4ever). The connections may not be obvious at first sight and their first choices weren't always available, but kids chose usernames that were in some way connected to themselves.

Next, Zoe explored Whyville and figured out how to earn money ("clams") so that she could customize her avatar. She quickly settled into a daily pattern: log in, check "ymail" messages (Whyville email), inspect her bank statement to see what she had earned, adjust her avatar's look, and then alternate between socializing with others and earning clams with an occasional shopping break for avatar parts at Akbar's Face Mall (see figure 2.1). In the early days of their lives in Whyville, players earn clams by playing science games; each level accomplished contributes one clam to one's salary, and players receive these salaries every time they log in to Whyville. So if a player has completed ten levels of various games, then she gets ten clams everyday she logs in. Very high salaries can get up to 130 to 160 clams per log-in. These clams can be used to purchase face parts (parts for one's avatar) in Whyville and occasionally to buy larger items like cars and houses.

Zoe gradually built up her salary by finishing several levels of science games, going through periods of heavier and lighter play of these games. She played salary-raising games frequently for the first few weeks on Whyville. Then she switched to other kinds of activities for a couple of weeks before apparently feeling the pinch of a low income, not having enough money to shop for her avatar. She played games more frequently again in the sixth through eighth weeks of her Whyville life. Playing science games in Whyville was a relatively minor aspect of kids' play overall, as it was more about earning clams than learning science. Achieving levels in the games was a means to an end as the clams earned gave kids more flexibility in customizing their avatars and hanging out with others. Thus,

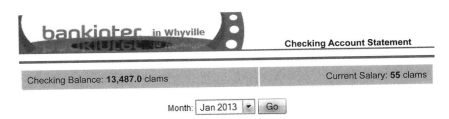

Checking Account Statement

Checking Balance: **13,487.0** clams   Current Salary: **55** clams

Month: | Jan 2013 ▼ | Go

Date	Transaction	Amount
Jan 30 7:48 AM	Whyville Salary	93
Jan 19 12:17 AM	WhyEat Bonus	25
Jan 18 12:11 AM	Ye Olde Projectile Shoppe	-100
Jan 14 10:35 AM	Ye Olde Projectile Shoppe	-20
Jan 9 9:29 AM	Whyville Salary	93
Jan 8 2:54 AM	Ackbar's Face Parts "R" Us	-68
Jan 4 3:19 AM	Oxygen Canister	-5
Jan 3 4:44 AM	Oxygen Canister	-5

Figure 2.1
Common places players visited, clockwise from upper left: City Beach, Bank Statement, Trading Post, and Akbar's Face Mall.

it is not surprising to see the relatively limited science games being picked up as activities for a short period of time and then left behind for more engaging activities. (An exception to this is the community-based science games that integrated socializing with science; for more on these, see chapters 6 and 7.) This in itself was an interesting discovery—playing socially with friends and creatively with avatar parts was more important to participants than playing short, educational mini-games.

In creating her avatar, bluwave, Zoe began like many players by using free parts from Grandma's Charity Bin, eventually supplementing these with parts gained from trades at the Trading Post or from shopping at Akbar's Face Mall. As she earned more clams (especially after her first two weeks), Zoe ceased going to Grandma's and relied solely on shopping and trading. This was a move toward higher competence in Whyville, as it meant developing a more socially acceptable look; parts from Grandma's are generally ill-esteemed and ridiculed as "newbie" looks (for more on this, see chapter 3). Shifting from Grandma's to Akbar's was a sign that Zoe and others were becoming insiders in Whyville.

By the end of her first week Zoe had already started a regular practice of browsing social areas in Whyville to try to make friends, jumping from space to space until she found people to talk with, whether a friend from school or new friends on Whyville. Once she made a new Whyville friend (usually in a highly populated area of Whyville like the beach), she would go with him or her to a quieter location to chat, then follow up the acquaintance by ymailing later. This was a common form of making friends: casual chatting in a crowded area, then chatting in a more private area, followed by sending a ymail. By the end of her first week Zoe had added flirting to her regular social agenda of making friends, a common practice we discuss in chapter 4.

Zoe's early patterns were similar to many other Whyvillians' for the first few weeks. Most club members kept up a similar pattern of logging in, looking for new ymail messages, checking their bank accounts, shopping for face parts, adjusting their avatars, and surfing Whyville to look for folks they knew or wanted to know. Yet the ordinariness of these patterns belies the challenges of adapting to an entirely new social environment; hidden beneath, one finds a variety of ways that members learned to speak new lingo, become financially established, look good, even to just get around— in all, to navigate life in Whyville.

Learning to Navigate Whyville

Once we understood some of the similarities in tweens' beginning days on Whyville, we went deeper into one particular area in order to unveil how club members were learning. Teleporting, for example, was an insider practice important to socializing on Whyville that could only be learned from another player.[8] Most places in Whyville are easy to access by means of the "Destination Menu," which allows Whyvillians to click on a pull-down menu in order to instantly transport to most locations in Whyville. However, the Destination Menu does not include some of the more popular places in which to socialize, such as Earth, Moon, Mars, Jupiter, Saturn, and the Newspaper. Because these sites are not listed in any written records on Whyville, the only way to discover them is through other people.[9] Therefore, these select places came to represent insider status and many players prized them as social hangouts because they were not overcrowded or over-populated by newbies (see figure 2.2).[10]

Teleporting was a practice that spread first slowly and then quickly in the after-school club over a period of two months, until all but one member

Figure 2.2
Visiting the Moon on Whyville.

knew how to teleport. The spread of the practice coincided with the club shifting from a quiet to a lively environment. At first, members played as partners on shared computers and occasionally asked the adult present for help when they needed something. Gradually members shifted from this isolated play to excited, collaborative gatherings in Whyville. As the tweens' participation in Whyville shifted to become more social, so did their interactions in the club. Instead of quietly playing a game by oneself or shopping for face parts with a friend sitting nearby, participants engaged more frequently in cross-club interactions: running between computers, high-fiving someone for a good mudball throw, and shouting across the room to "Go to the Mall!" or "Meet me at the Moon!" These types of cross-space social interactions really took hold during the fourth and fifth weeks of the club, so it should not be a surprise that almost half of the club members teleported for the first time during those weeks when knowledge about the command and the new locations spread like wildfire from one member to another.

As tweens called across the room, others inevitably became curious about the places being talked about, like the Moon. They solicited knowledge about teleporting in a variety of ways: asking friends in person in the club, asking friends in Whyville, even asking strangers in Whyville. Consider the rather complicated situation that prompted Gabe to learn how to teleport. He and Briana were sitting at adjacent computers, yet hanging out in different places in Whyville. A strange avatar said hi to Gabe by his last name ("hi smith"), and Gabe called Briana over to ask if she knew who that person was. Briana exclaimed with delight that it was their classmate, Marv. Marv told Gabe to "go to the moon," a place that was just beginning to become a cool hangout among club members.

The following conversation ensued:

Briana: Teleport to the moon!
Gabe: Okay, I don't know how to though.
Briana: No no wait, hold on.
Gabe: You teleport me there, please [asking Briana to type it for him, which she did not do]…
Gabe: "Let's go to the moon" [reading out loud Marv's second request to go to the Moon]. Okay. [Gabe types "ok."]
Gabe: Hey how do you teleport to the moon?
Briana: Write, write that. Teleport moon.
Gabe: Okay.

Gabe: Tel-e-port [typing as he talks].
Briana: Don't write "to" just write "teleport moon," m-o-o-n [spelling Moon].
Gabe: Teleport moon [types].

Over the course of a few minutes Briana explained to Gabe how to teleport to the moon, being careful to correct his syntax when he began typing "teleport to the moon" instead of correctly writing "teleport moon." This example showcases a common type of collaborative play in the club, where one member would hang over the shoulder of another to look at the computer screen—demonstrating some of the openness of the tools (computer screens) and the space of the club.[11] It is also an example of the "periodic monitoring" we have previously seen among peers teaching each other, keeping an eye on one another's work and correcting as necessary.[12]

Teleporting illustrates the many resources used by club members in learning how to play in Whyville. All but three club members learned through a combination of different social and material resources: from friends in the club, friends in their class, friends in Whyville, strangers in Whyville, or observations of friends on their computers. Once tweens learned how to teleport to one location, they often engaged in trial-and-error exploration of where they could go. For instance, Leslie rattled off a string of teleport commands to several locations, discovering that the Earth and Saturn were locations in Whyville, while Venus and Pluto were not: "teleport moon, teleport mars, teleport venus, teleport earth, teleport pluto, teleport saturn." Not only this, but once members learned how to teleport, they taught other Whyvillians how to teleport. Whenever conversations came up online about teleporting, they were almost always in situations where a club member was teaching someone else how to teleport. Half of these conversations were between club members, but the other half were with Whyvillians at large, demonstrating the ways that members began to socialize with (and teach!) the broader Whyville community beyond their known friends.

Zoe's Pathways into Whyville

Thus far we have largely discussed common activities among Whyvillians, especially club members. While it is true that there are many common activities in Whyville—everyone checks their bank statements, plays games, and most learn how to teleport—Whyville is vast and allows kids to develop their own personal pathways to participation in the virtual world. Here we turn back to Zoe to understand the ways that she found her own personal way in Whyville and how this developed over time.

The Trading Post

One of the places where Zoe spent extensive amounts of time in Whyville was the Trading Post, a kind of eBay-like spot, where Whyvillians traded face parts in order to earn clams or find sold-out face parts. In the after-school club, Zoe was one of the first members to teach others how to trade in Whyville, and she often solicited friends to go to the Trading Post and trade with her. In an interview, she said that one of her favorite parts about Whyville was trading, as it related to the financial exploration she enjoyed in Whyville. How did she figure out how to trade well, and what were her activities at the Trading Post?

Zoe first went to the Trading Post on her second day in Whyville. In her first week, Zoe spent eight hours at the Trading Post, where she quickly learned to trade efficiently. At first she spoke in long phrases such as "does anyone want a head?" or "okay, ill trade the pokadot hair pin for the clams." But by her the end of her first week she had adapted to a shortened, more precise language that fit her trading interests. Consider the differences between two different trading exchanges on Day 3 and Day 6:

Day 3	Day 6
you have anything else?	u lik
let me see!!	a barrette for your hair
some clams	HI!
okay, ill trade the pokadot hair pin for the clams	25??
	Kk
ill trade the clamz for the hair	how about 20
let me see!	
yes..the first one looks cool!!!!	
wanta trade	

These trade negotiations show how important it was to learn the new language in Whyville. In the second trade (Day 5), we can see that Zoe was already using shorter invitations and abbreviations ("u lik"), a sales pitch ("a barrette for your hair"), and cut-to-the-chase negotiations for clams, which she realized were more versatile than face parts ("25?? ... how about 20"). Within just one week she had learned an insider practice in Whyville.

In addition to changing her language use, Zoe also changed the way she utilized the Trading Post. Instead of engaging in longer conversations with Whyvillians in a given room in the Post, she learned to use the space more efficiently by cycling quickly from room to room saying, "u lik?" or "got any clamz?" and quickly moving on to another room if she did not like the answers. This probably made better use of her time, allowing her to see more people in a shorter amount of time and quickly ascertain whether they were potential trading partners. All of these changes in participation exhibit Zoe's quick learning of how to play in a specific area of Whyville: navigating spaces, understanding financial negotiations, understanding what was valuable, and speaking the language.[13] The Trading Post was uniquely important to Zoe in other ways as well. She made her first Whyville friends there, experienced rejection and acceptance, and learned what was considered ugly and "hot" on Whyville. It was also a place where she explored further how to connect aspects of her personal identity to her Whyville avatar, which we will discuss in more detail in chapter 3.

Shifting to Checkers

Yet the Trading Post was not always a part of Zoe's Whyville life. After three months of intense engagement there, she shifted her play to beauty contests, trivia contests, and checkers, all of which could be seen as competitive social pursuits like trading was. Beauty contests consisted of spontaneously held contests where one Whyvillian would announce a contest and ask interested contestants to line up. The contest holder would then decide who was the most "hot," pretty, or cute, and proclaim that individual the winner, often offering clams as a reward for winning. Trivia contests took place in the Greek Theater, a place where Whyvillians could gather and sit in an amphitheater-style arena while someone up front would ask questions. Checkers was one of several multiplayer games on Whyville (which include mancala and Chinese checkers). She began playing checkers for up to forty minutes at a time, complaining bitterly when her opponent was too nice and refused to "jump" over her pieces. Checkers replaced the Trading Post as the place where she had personal conversations about race (Zoe said she was black), made friends, and shared insults or compliments depending on the interaction. Checkers continued to be a prime social spot for Zoe until the end of our observations, six months after she began playing on Whyville.

Pathways of Other Players into Whyville

Of course, other players had different patterns of play in Whyville, each developing their own personal trajectories into Whyville and finding their own way into activities that were more interesting to them. Here we take the opportunity to introduce our remaining five case study tweens from the club whose Whyville lives we researched in great depth. We will return to them and Zoe throughout the book.

Briana/whskr29

Twelve-year old Briana loved to chat with others in Whyville—both friends from school and new Whyvillians that she met. She talked extensively with school pals online about homework, friends, and general "who liked whom" gossip, but she spoke just as frequently with Whyvillians. This socializing formed the core of her interest on Whyville and was one reason why she quickly learned things that were new to other club members. She was one of the first people in the club to learn how to teleport and throw projectiles, which is why she was positioned to teach Gabe how to teleport. This expertise helped her learn to play science games that other club members never fully learned, like the Zero Gravity game where one had to throw something in one direction in order to move in the opposite direction (demonstrating Newton's laws). Briana was also one of the first to design her own face parts (see chapter 3) and to make additional avatars that allowed her to play with her identity as well as earn double or triple salaries every day. Yet once the club ended, Briana rarely went on Whyville. It would seem that the socialization with her friends was important enough to her that she had little motivation to go on once the physical social space was no longer active.

Brad/vulcan61

Brad, ten years old, joined the club several weeks late, but this meant that he was able to build on his friends' expertise to catch up quickly in Whyville. Within days he was engaging in activities that had taken others weeks to learn: teleporting, throwing projectiles, and flirting. He especially enjoyed meeting with other boys in the club on Whyville to engage in throwing wars, meeting in one place to throw snowballs, mudballs, and maggots at each other in boisterous play (see chapter 4). Brad spent more time engaged in face-related activities (shopping for and adjusting his avatar) than any other activity, and chatted a lot with others. He took up a pattern of speeding quickly through Whyville, jumping from place to place in rapid succession, sometimes spending only seconds in each place. Sometimes this meant cycling through as many as sixty to seventy places in just eight to ten minutes—speedy indeed! This served as a way to scan locales in Whyville and find friends he recognized, Whyvillians who looked interesting, or anyone at all. It's also probably the reason why "teleport" was by far his most frequently typed word, as he teleported quite often while scanning places to find friends.

Isabel/ivy06

On the surface, ten-year-old Isabel was an average player. She shopped, played games, built up her salary, and played with other club members. However, a closer look revealed that flirting was one of her most dominant social activities in Whyville. At first, her flirting was just like all the other club members, with just a comment here and there to get a boyfriend. Interestingly, in the beginning many Whyvillians perceived her avatar to be a boy, and many girls flirted with her in that capacity. Isabel embraced this for a while and experimented with flirting as a guy to get girlfriends. Then later she developed a more feminine Whyville appearance and sought out boyfriends. Of course, flirting wasn't Isabel's only activity—she actually spent more time on shopping than anything else.

Aiden/masher47

Twelve-year-old Aiden epitomized a casual socializer in the club and in Whyville. In the club, Aiden bragged loudly about his flirting, while girls provided criticism on his pickup lines. Like many of the other boys he also loved projectile mudball fights, and a few times this even resulted in some friendly roughhousing in the club after someone hit him with a mudball in Whyville. His favorite spot in Whyville was the beach, where he struck up friendships, tried out countless pickup lines on cute girls, and played with his friends from the club. In fact, by far the two most frequently used words he said were "Hey" and "Hi," an indication of just how often he greeted people, though he rarely continued conversations much past an initial greeting.

Blake/raybeams

Nine-year-old Blake turned out to be one of the more intense players on Whyville, though he did not begin that way. Like Brad, he socialized frequently but shallowly, engaging in short conversations with lots of people, organizing projectile fights among club members, occasionally flirting, and regularly boasting of these flirtations in the club. His conversation shifted seamlessly between chatting with friends like Brad in Whyville and in the club, and between conversations with school friends and flirting with or throwing projectiles at other Whyvillians. Yet after the club ended, Blake suddenly began investing more time in Whyville in ways that focused on clams. He raised his salary through science games, spent days designing and producing face parts in the Face Factory, and finally began trading in rare parts. Friendships from school continued to be a strong part of his Whyville life, but shifted alongside his new activities, as friends asked him to design specific parts for them and debated how many he should produce so as not to flood the Whyville market. Thus, even when Blake was exploring the high end of Whyville finance, he remained rooted in his everyday relationships with people he knew.

Whyville Players Writ Large

Thus far we have described Whyville players from the after-school club we ran in early 2005, going deep into the six case studies we chose from our group of twenty tweens. But these case studies reflect aspects of Whyville players writ large. To understand the overall patterns of kids' participation in Whyville, we took our larger sample of tweens (595 of them[14]) and analyzed every click they made and every word of chat they typed. A few things stand out. First, there were indeed common activities. In fact, the most dominant activity of all Whyville players involved avatars. Whyvillians spent more than one-third of their time customizing their avatars—shopping, dressing, editing, trading, and designing.[15] Whether boys or girls, experienced or inexperienced, they all devoted large chunks of time (and virtual money) to this creative enterprise. Though it is not surprising that personalizing one's look was an important aspect of being online—after all, it is the basis on which people make many initial judgments—we were surprised by how just how prominent an activity this was.

Second, very few differences in activities were found to be based on gender. We decided to see if girls, who dominate the Whyville scene (67 percent of players), played any differently than boys. Essentially they did not. Boys tended to play a few more multiplayer games or focus on economic activities (e.g., looking at their bank accounts) a bit more often, but these differences were quite slim,[16] especially considering that these activities were relatively minor parts of Whyville life compared with other activities like hanging out in social spots, chatting, ymailing, and of course creating avatars. This too surprised us because in the after-school club we had certainly noticed differences in how kids played online. For instance, we were under the impression that throwing projectiles and flirting were primarily boys' activities. Yet when we looked at members' online activities, we discovered that girls participated in throwing projectiles and flirting just as much (and sometimes more) than the boys. The only difference was that they did not advertise these activities in the club, saying more about the gendered space of the club as promoting differences between play than the space of Whyville. We will explore these two activities more in chapter 4.

So finally we looked to see if there were any differences at all between Whyville players, and indeed there were.[17] The major difference between Whyvillians was how much time they spent overall in Whyville. The most heavily involved players, the "Core" players, formed a very small percentage of Whyvillians overall: only 7 percent. Next was the group of "Average" players (34 percent), and finally, by far the largest group, whom we call the "Casual" players (59 percent). The Core players spent by far the most time on Whyville, and perhaps not surprisingly this group spent much more time socializing, chatting, ymailing, and customizing avatars than any other group. Average players took part in far fewer activities than the Core tier, but they also engaged in more science games, economic activities, and social hanging out than the Casual players (see also figure 2.3).

This begins to give us a picture of players on Whyville. The most engaged players perform activities that are intrinsic parts of the culture of Whyville, being very social and playing creatively with their looks. In contrast, the mini-science games that formed a key part of Average players' activities have design limits—one can only play until one has finished the game. Core players likely finished all or most of the science games and proceeded to spend the majority of their time hanging out and designing avatars. Those design activities, unlike most of the mini-science games, can

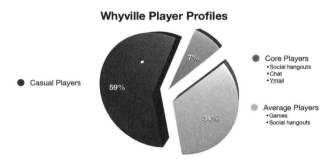

Whyville Player Profiles

Casual Players — 59%

7% — Core Players
• Social hangouts
• Chat
• Ymail

34% — Average Players
• Games
• Social hangouts

Figure 2.3
Distribution of player types.

continue for a long time without needing the designers to make new games or levels. Such design activities also tap more explicitly into creative play, which online participation can foster.

Our case-study tweens from the club fit into these categories of players. Zoe and Blake are part of the Core players—not surprising, since they found ways to play creatively through trading and designing face parts and playing socially through long conversations with friends at the Trading Post, Beach, or Checkers games. Isabel and Brad fit into the Average player group. They pursued enough science games to raise their salaries and engaged in socializing, but never quite to the degree that Zoe and Blake did. Finally, Aiden and Briana were part of the Casual players. For both youths, once the club ended they spent much less time on Whyville. Though Briana probably played more science games than any other club member, this was limited by the number of available games to play and though she certainly played with club members and many Whyvillians, she simply did not engage in the same levels of play as Zoe and Blake.

Many other online communities have found similar patterns of participation in their player groups. Only a small majority of participants in online social communities participate in the most visible activities.[18] In fact, although it is popular to refer to current young people as "digital natives,"[19] several scholars question this term. In their research on large groups of college-age young adults who have grown up with the Internet, Esther Hargittai and Gina Walejko[20] have found that only a small number of people actually participate in creating content and sharing it online. Those that do are likely to have parents with higher levels of education. In their extensive ethnography of youth who participate in online activities, Mizuko Ito and colleagues[21] referred to three different modes of interaction online: "hanging out, messing around, and geeking out." Relatively few kids actually participated in the activities deemed to be most productive educationally online: "geeking out" through making and sharing knowledge, videos, photographs, blogs, and the like. As in Whyville, a large amount of online traffic is generated by a relatively small group of players who are the most visible because of these high levels of activity. It is important to look not just to the most involved players, but to the entire range of players to understand what kids are getting out of the participation in different online sites.

Looking at tweens' play in Whyville provides a fascinating lens onto how kids learn to participate in a new social environment, both online and offline. Whyville is, well, different. Over the years it has developed its own unique culture, as any social place does, be it a school, church, family, community group, or virtual world. Each has its own unique local culture where certain activities, words, and ways of interacting are valued and fostered. Studying how kids learned to participate in Whyville can help us understand how kids learn to participate in other environments as well and provide a better foundation for designing and supporting learning and teaching activities in virtual worlds.

In the next chapters we will delve into tweens' participation in particular Whyville activities more extensively: how kids played creatively with identity through avatar designs (chapter 3), how they explored friendships (romantic and otherwise) (chapter 4), and how they played with various moral issues like cheating and scamming (chapter 5). These chapters continue to build on the theme of our book of virtual worlds as social playgrounds for kids, connected but different from other spaces of their everyday lives.

3   Identity Play

Hello I'm Tami324 reporting live at Whyville. Over 1/2 of the Whyville avatar population is white faced, but 1/3 of the population have a black face. But what's interesting is that most black faces don't have bodies or if they do have bodies, they are white. Now I'm not saying that anyone in Whyville is exactly racist, but we do have the tendency to only make bodies for white faced avatars. What I'm saying is that there are faces other than white ones and we shound remember that. I am trying to produce a whole line of products for black avatars and I would appreciate it if some of you out there would help. I already have some people working on designs but we need more! If anyone could possibly spare some clams to give to this project or make a piece yourself, please contact me about it through Y-Mail. So if you are donating clams or making a piece I can record it so people will get the proper credit.

Please Please Please think about this cause and see if you can support it!

—Tami324[1]

When Zoe was first developing her "look" on Whyville, by which we mean her 2D cartoonlike avatar, she began with the stock parts available for free at Grandma's. Grandma's is Whyville's equivalent of a thrift store where newcomers especially can get donated goods. Other Whyvillians poked fun at her, saying "Oh you newbie face, you need to buy clothes that the girls wear." This was one of Zoe's first realizations that she did not fit in on Whyville. Apparently, her first avatar was just a face with no neck and no clothes. So she made an effort to get more parts that looked "like me," as she explained in a later interview.

Even in her first week Zoe began to pursue an African-American look on Whyville, what she meant by "like me." Clearly her ethnicity and skin color were important to who she wanted to be in Whyville, tied into her identity on that site. She began by getting a face that was dark brown, but she had difficulty finding clothes that matched. We saw this in her repeated requests for shirts that matched her dark-skinned head beginning on her fourth day in Whyville (January 14): "does anyone hav any african-ameri-can t-shirts???" In Whyville, all clothing comes with necks, so an African-American T-shirt is a shirt with a dark brown neck and arms. One fashion faux pas is to have a neck that does not match one's head—it is something of a jarring look as the squared-off top of the neck juts into the rounded face.

Yet dark-skinned clothes are difficult to find. In fact, we counted all the faces and clothes available on Whyville and documented that indeed there were nearly nine times more peach-skinned parts than there were dark brown, lighter brown, olive, or yellow-skinned parts in Whyville's shop-ping mall. It is actually quite difficult to obtain non-peach-colored bodies and clothes.[2] Zoe initially struggled with these inequities in her efforts to obtain dark-skinned bodies to match her head, but she persevered none-theless. She frequented the Trading Post, repeatedly asking for "black" or "african-american" face parts. Often, people offered to trade clothes with peach skin, to which she replied, "no i'm not white" or "do u have any black ones?" To which some Whyvillians responded by holding up a black-colored t-shirt with peach skin. "No! not that kind of black! african-ameri-can," Zoe replied. Clearly her pursuit to be herself by being ethnically black on Whyville was not an easy one and took its toll.

At the beginning of her fourth week in Whyville, Zoe shifted her approach. Instead of eagerly soliciting dark-skinned face parts she began to apologize for only having African-American parts when she began a trade: "2 tell u the truth … i don't hav the type of stuff … do u mind if it's african-american?" Not long after this shift, she suddenly decided to switch from trading African-American parts to only dealing in "Latino" parts, denoting a lighter shade of brown that was more easily obtained in Whyville. In an interview, she referred to this Latino look, saying it "didn't look a lot like me." Yet at the same time this look represented an achievement for Zoe. Whyvillians no longer made fun of her looks. She had successfully created an avatar that may not have been "African-American" but had darker skin than most Whyvillians and had other creative elements that were meaning-ful to her—angel wings, a T-shirt with her sister's name on it, and an arm to rest her chin on when she was bored.

Zoe's development of her avatar shows some of the many tensions tweens face in representing themselves online. Many want to *connect* to aspects of themselves in other areas of their lives—their ethnicity, gen-der, hobbies, interests, relationships, even political priorities.[3] But within

Whyville, as within other virtual worlds, there are social standards of what looks good, as well as powers, resources, and tools that affect how one can look. Indeed, as Beth Kolko has pointed out, creating one's identity online is an exploration of relations between power, culture, and the individual.[4] Learning these social protocols and utilizing digital tools effectively in order to meet them (or even choosing to reject those values) while still representing oneself in a personal way is an achievement that should not be taken for granted in Whyville —or in "real life," either.

Playing with Identity

More than twenty-five years ago, Sherry Turkle wrote the influential book *The Second Self: Computers and the Human Spirit*,[5] where she introduced the idea that computers could be sites for exploring oneself and building an identity, rather than just for work and calculations. In her next book, *Life on the Screen: Identity in the Age of the Internet*,[6] she expanded these ideas specifically to online games where players could assume different identities by adopting a fictive name or gender.[7] Players now have a great degree of flexibility in creating their avatars, their alternate online-world-based identities, through customizable images as well as usernames. Indeed, a popular idea has surfaced that on the Internet, one can be anyone one wants to be, without limitations.

An avatar is one's representation of oneself in a social world, an idea that is closely linked to the concept of identity. Erik Erikson popularized identity (and the term "identity crisis") as an important developmental stage in adolescence where youth explore and figure out who they are.[8] The development of identity plays an important role as kids decide which groups they identify with, what kind of persons they wish to be within those groups, and what is required to become those persons.[9] From this point of view, creating an avatar and establishing oneself in a virtual world can be part of exploring identities. Many researchers agree that the same issues that adolescents face in their everyday lives (school, family, friends) also persist in online social environments. Adolescents explore aspects of their gender, ethnicity, sexuality, personal interests, and other areas of their personality online just as they work to figure out these aspects of themselves offline. For instance, it is well known that a main topic of adolescents' talk and activity concerns romantic relationships; they pursue these topics in online chat rooms[10] and virtual worlds just as they do in their everyday

lives with friends (see chapter 4 for more on this topic). Similarly, understanding one's ethnic identity is important for youth,[11] and recent studies
on online social networking sites demonstrate that youth try to understand
who they are in relation to others of different ethnicities in those spaces as
well as in their everyday lives.[12] For Zoe and others we describe later in this
chapter, learning how to be black in Whyville was an important part of
their identity exploration.

Yet as may be apparent from Zoe's often frustrated attempts to make the
kind of avatar she wanted, avatars and identities are made within social
environments where people and digital tools play a role in shaping who one
can be. This idea draws on a sociocultural perspective on identity, a viewpoint where one's identity is created not just within oneself but through
interaction with others over time.[13] We act differently with different people
because of the ways that others shape how we interact and who we are.
Different groups of people have different values, attitudes, ways of talking,
and even ways of looking. The same is true in Whyville and other virtual
worlds as well as in classrooms, within families, in jobs, and so on. Social
factors within Whyville interacted with Zoe's own desires in shaping how
she developed her avatar. Her looks were created within design constraints
(including a lack of dark-skinned clothing) and social constraints (what
looks good, what others value, etc.). Even though her initial avatar's looks
fulfilled her desire to look African-American, they did not meet aesthetic
standards within Whyville, and after pushback from others, Zoe progres-
sively altered her look in response to Whyvillian standards of acceptability
while still reflecting her own personality.

The design tools in virtual worlds allow different degrees of freedoms in
creating avatars, from Second Life's nearly unlimited design tools for making three-dimensional avatars, to Whyville's broad tools to draw and layer
two-dimensional face parts, to Club Penguin's standard penguin avatar that
can be accessorized with premade clothes, hats, jewelry, and badges. In-
game currency and accomplishments (e.g., leveling up in a game) often
allow players access to special accessories, so that one's avatar can show off
one's expertise in the virtual world. For many players, avatars are far from
ephemeral and spurious creations; players spend considerable time selecting and customizing them before interacting with others online.[14] Because
no roles or races are assigned (unlike in online role-playing games), players
have a choice to create avatars that resemble who they are in real life or to
make very different kinds of avatars (blue orbs of light, carrots, soda cups,

animals). Strikingly, though, most players choose to be human[15] and relatively attractive[16] in worlds where they could allegedly be anything.

Virtual worlds like Second Life and Whyville stand out among many others because they allow members to make and sell their own self-designed avatar parts. Indeed, in Whyville, virtually all of the 30,000 face parts available for sale are made by kids for kids.[17] Designing "face parts" in Whyville is a challenging process where kids draw two-dimensional images using a select palette of colors, price them, and pay a manufacturing fee per part they produce. While they can produce unlimited numbers of their designs (if they have enough clams up front), they can also play the market to create limited edition items at high prices. Beyond this they can create and advertise stores to sell their own designs or collaborate with others to create a store that represents several designers. One of the challenges for virtual worlds that allow players to make their own avatars or avatar parts is that the design tools can be very difficult to use effectively; many people give up early on in the process of making and selling avatar parts.[18] But those who do not design their own avatar parts enjoy great freedom in selecting from tens of thousands of parts in making their avatars.

Anatomy of an Avatar

Whyville avatars are difficult to understand without actually seeing them, so here we unpack some of the symbolic significance in tweens' choices in avatar design. We present two avatars from our 2008 after-school club where we carefully documented each avatar at the end of every day so that we could see how they changed over time. Figures 3.1 and 3.2 show two illustrations of Whyville avatars, from Taylor (twelve-year-old Caucasian girl) and Ben (twelve-year-old Indian American boy). These are the avatars they developed at least two months after starting on Whyville and they show some of the common Whyville trends.

Taylor's avatar has an oversized rainbow hat, layers two separate hair pieces (pink over dark brown), and accessorizes with a Gryffindor tie (showing interest in the Harry Potter series), angel wings, and other clothing (overalls, white T-shirt). Ben, who received fashion assistance from Lucetta in designing his avatar, has a more masculine oversized hat with two insignia (one from Whyville, one a brand name) loosely floating over his hat. He has a pet and a skateboard, and his outfit is all one piece (a gray jacket with a tie). Both of these tweens fit in very well on Whyville with these looks, which consist of eleven to twelve separate parts and took quite a bit of time and effort to develop. They demonstrate the sophistication of developing a good-looking avatar in Whyville, and the financial, design, and other resources needed to accomplish this. At the same time they also show aspects of each individual's personality, especially if one probes into the decisions made with each piece that was layered on.

To understand how tweens develop their avatars over time we turn to Lucetta and her journey of avatar development, which shares some similarities to Zoe's. Lucetta was also a twelve-year-old girl at the time of the club, with mixed white/Irish American and black/Honduran roots.[19] She loved fashion; one of the things she liked most about Whyville was that "I could change my look ... I like buying stuff and then changing it." In the beginning when she selected her first Whyville avatar from a preset menu of choices, she said, "At first I was trying to put, get my person to kind of look like me." Her first avatar had dark and curly hair, dark skin, and brown eyes (see image 1 in figure 3.3). Then she went shopping for the first time and bought the first black hair she could find (again sticking to trying to look like herself—see image 2). As she began to have more money she could afford more items, so she bought a headband (3–5) and a flower to put on the headband. She also bought new clothes (the white outfit in 3) which required a matching face. Both the face and clothes had a slightly lighter but still very similar skin tone. She experimented with different eyes, eventually settling on some new blue eyes that she kept for a couple of months

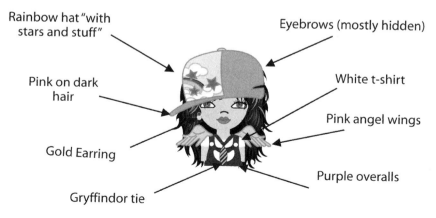

Figure 3.1
Taylor's avatar.

(5). As is visible in image 4, she also played with the placement of eyes, mouth, lips and nose. A common look in Whyville is to have the eyes low on one's head with the lips almost at the bottom of one's chin.

Lucetta eventually got several new items—a striped top (7), a stuffed elephant (7), sunglasses (7, 9), a belt (6, 10, 12), a new flower for her hair (9, 10), and earrings (10, 12). She changed these items nearly every day, just as she would wear different outfits everyday to school or events.

We held a costume contest in the club during one week where she dressed as a bald, green alien (8), described in full in chapter 7 in this book. She bought a new outfit that meant she needed a new, lighter skinned face (9), which she kept on her avatar afterward, shifting further away from looking like herself. Cementing this shift, she and her friend Taylor were shopping at the same time and saw two pieces of hair that they both liked. "We decided ta, one would get one and one would get the other. And then, if we wanted to, we could switch." Just like friends sharing clothes in real life (which Taylor and Lucetta couldn't do very easily because they wore very different sizes), they planned on sharing outfits in Whyville. One day she and Taylor also played at being a devil (Lucetta—see image 11 in figure 3.3) and an angel (Taylor), the same day that Whyville officials duct-taped Lucetta for revealing in Whyville where she went to school. Duct-taping is a disciplinary measure that is taken by Whyville officials when kids say things that are either offensive or share information deemed too private. She laughed about the duct-tape over her mouth all day in the club.

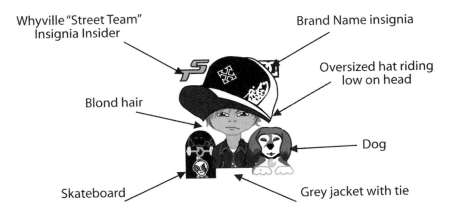

Figure 3.2
Ben's avatar.

Lucetta and Zoe share several common themes with other members of the after-school club. At the beginning, most kids wanted to look like themselves and chose looks that were similar to their skin color, hair color, and eye color. They slowly changed their initial looks with affordable parts as their income grew in Whyville, allowing them greater flexibility in making their avatars. They also began to exhibit the tacit ideas of "good looks" in Whyville, with greatly accessorized avatars, placement of eyes and eyebrows, oversized hats, lips low on the chin, and so on. Eventually, most kids who began with darker shades of skin eventually migrated to lighter-skinned looks. For Zoe, this meant being Latina. For Briana, this meant becoming a pixie (purple skin); for Lucetta and many others, this meant having peach/white skin.

The trend away from darker skin tones in many of the club members is troubling and highlights the way that racial inequity often persists online,[20] even in places where one can allegedly "be" whoever one wants. Zoe, Briana, and Tyrone were especially aware of the choices they made to step away from looking "African-American" on Whyville. Yet each found the means to express their ethnic identity in other ways. Briana and Zoe hung out at Geek Speak, what is popularly known as "the black place" in Whyville among citizens and where kids' chat is influenced by black vernacular English and hip hop. Tyrone made sure that others on Whyville knew that he was not white, as his avatar might lead people to believe, since it was a pale-skinned figure based on popular Japanese anime figures. As he wrote on his profile page, "I'm white here but I'm actually a 12 year old black kid." This is not to say that his avatar did not represent him—it drew on motifs from popular Japanese anime series like *Naruto* in which he was keenly interested. But it did not fully represent who he was.

Just as face parts are layered together to make avatars, we can think of avatars as laminated[21] with meanings that reflect the individual's interests, aspects of identity, resources available, and the local cultures in which the avatars are built. We say "cultures," plural rather than singular, because oftentimes avatars are shared across spaces—kids occupy Whyville at the same time that they may play with friends they know in school or their neighborhood. Their avatar designs reflect values from each of these worlds. This is *connected* identity play, where identity expression meets with limited resources and social dynamics across multiple worlds, a tension discussed regularly in Whyville's weekly periodical, the *Whyville Times*.

1 - April 4

2 - April 7

3 - April 11

4 - April 10

5 - April 21

6 - April 25

7 - May 4

8 - May 6
Costume Costume

9 - May 12

10 - May 16

11 - May 23

12 - June 2

Figure 3.3
Lucetta's avatar development in the costume contest.

Looking Good in a Virtual World: A Tween Community View

By and large, Whyvillians discuss the challenges to making good avatars that represent themselves on a regular basis. The weekly serial the *Whyville Times*, written by Whyvillians and lightly edited by Whyville's host Numedeon, forms one of the main areas for community discussion on important issues in the virtual world. Fashion and avatars feature strongly in the paper—in no fewer than 587 articles over the past seven years Whyvillians discussed "face parts." That's nearly two articles per week! In these articles, tween authors write, advise, critique, and plead for activism concerning Whyville avatar fashion—like Tami324's article quoted in this chapter's introduction.

In large part, articles on face parts advise newcomers on how to look good: what parts to buy, where to shop, and how *not* to dress. Having eyebrows is good, but layering eyebrows on *top* of hair rather than underneath is uncouth. Having a neck that doesn't match one's head is inadvisable. And for goodness sake, please, please accessorize: sunglasses, hair add-ons, bandanas, hats, just accessorize. Many authors also share tips about designing face parts and getting through the administrative red tape to get those designs approved for sale (designs must meet Numedeon approval and not show brands, breasts, or profanity). Some criticize Akbar's Face Mall (the prime shopping spot for all things avatar) for excluding their designs, delaying approval, or posing constraints on what was allowed.

Yet not all Whyvillians are consumed by what looks good or the logistics of making and selling parts. Quite a number of authors are concerned with using face parts for a cause, encouraging originality instead of popularity, confronting discrimination against the less good-looking, and even crying for equal racial representation. Whyvillians use their avatars not only to express their personality but also to advertise favorite causes. It should not be surprising that when citizens have a cause to fight for (such as saving the town of Whyville or saving the environment), they would support it sartorially. After all, appearance is one of the primary forms of self-expression and design in Whyville, and citizens use this agency in much the same way fashion is used for social and political action in real life (think of all the T-shirts that advertise various causes).

As hinted at in the life of Zoe's avatar, many Whyvillians make fun of those whose avatars do not meet common community standards. This

Eyebrows above the hair.

No eyebrows

Too big of a nose

Misuse of contact lenses

Mismatched head & body

Mismatched head & body

Figure 3.4
Fashion faux pas in Whyville.

discrimination largely falls along class lines as newbies have less money to buy face parts. Yet many writers in the *Whyville Times* take a stand against those who make fun of others for unusual looks. Challenging pressures to look a certain way, one anonymous author said:

To meet a person with the courage to stand out and express him or her self with face parts is very rare to find these days. ... Have variety in your appearance! Take advantage of life and the choice of so many face parts![22]

Comments like this both recognize and push back against the cultural norms in Whyville. Members become aware of these norms very quickly (as Zoe did when she was made fun of), but voices for welcoming rather than bullying and for originality rather than conformity do exist.

Social Activism through Avatars

Tator Day!   One way that these welcoming voices triumphed in Whyville was through citizens' popular interpretations of a computer glitch that came to be known as Tator Day. The history of Tator Day is an interesting one. Until 2007, newbies on Whyville were given smiley faces when they created an account and were often given the derogatory nickname "tator," probably because the faces look like oblong potatoes. Occasional glitches in the server that stored face parts sometimes caused all faces on Whyville to resort back to the newbie, or tator, face. These events came to be known and written about as "Tator Day." Although it was unintentional on the designers' part, many Whyvillians began to celebrate Tator Day as an equalizing event where the rich and poor, popular and unpopular, newbies and oldies were no longer distinguishable. As one Whyvillian wrote in the *Whyville Times*:

Even though this day may not have been intentional or sent by the City Workers, even though it may have been just a computer glitch, I still grasp it as a day of acceptance, for many people. This day may just slightly bridge the gaps between all the stereotypes in Whyville.[23]

In fact, while some complained about losing their face parts for a day, many Whyvillians enjoyed Tator Day as a community event, collaboratively posing for pictures (see figure 3.5), playing practical jokes (telling people who just logged on that they were the only ones who had newbie faces and they had lost all their face parts), and generally greeting each other with "Happy Tator Day."

Figure 3.5
Tator Day in Whyville.

Further activism surrounding racial representation on Whyville led to two site-wide changes in the avatars available for newbies. Up until early 2006, newbies were given peach-colored smiley faces for their first avatars. After protests from authors in the *Whyville Times*, and in fact in response to a specific suggestion by one author, Numedeon changed the smiley face color from peach to blue. A year or so later, Whyville provided new citizens multiple options for their initial avatar, including six choices each for heads (in a range of realistic skin tones), noses, hair, bodies, eyes, and mouths. In this way, pressure from the tween populace actually affected top-down changes by the designers. Yet because so much of the responsibility for design is left with players in Whyville, someone needed to incite them to action too.

Blacks Deserve Bodies Too! The quote by Kerri_87 at the beginning of this chapter comes from an activist article she wrote calling citizens to tackle the problem of racial equity in Whyville by designing more diverse body parts. Her complaint about the lack of body parts available to coordinate with the limited supply of brown and tan heads was not an isolated sentiment. Regular articles addressing this concern appeared over a period of two years from 2000 to 2002. Several authors echoed Kerri_87's call for community action, including Liss22, who wrote the following in her 2002 article, "Racism, Clothes, and City Workers":

What you need to realize is that it's not the Workers, but the citizens who have taken the most active role in the DESIGNING of face parts. ... Complaining and blaming the general public because of the lack of dark skinned outfits isn't helping anything; you can't order people to make parts for you, and they have no obligation to do so. The logical thing, obviously, is design it for yourself. Instead of telling us we could get rich off of making dark skinned clothes, take advantage of your own advice—YOU could.

Like Kerri_87, Liss22 is very clear in locating the responsibility for the lack of diversity in face-part colors in the hands of Whyvillians themselves. The role of player-generated content in Whyville certainly opens up a unique role for citizens to change what tools are available to them for crafting an online identity, and Liss22 and others like her played a vocal role in convincing citizens to design face parts in more colors.

In 2003, the tone of the public discussion of head and body colors shifted when one of the original six critics of the lack of variety in part colors, Tike, published a news article (Tike 2003) proclaiming that the situation had improved, thanks to entrepreneurial trendsetting citizens:

To be direct about it, citizens believed that there was a limited amount of clothing made especially for ethnic groups. Most clothes were directed towards Caucasian individuals. ... I am here to report that things have changed, thanks to those designers who took a chance and began creating face parts with different skin tones. Some even began the trend by wearing their parts so that others would catch on and purchase them. Even those who do not necessarily have darker skin outside of Whyville choose to wear items of this sort.

It is possible that Whyvillians as a whole agreed with Tike's satisfaction in the improved variety of available non-peach parts, because no further complaints about face part color were aired in the *Whyville Times* for a few years. However, there continues to be a relatively short supply of non-peach bodies to choose from. So, although the current situation may be an improvement from 2000 to 2002 conditions, it is still not as easy to assemble a brown, olive, or yellow look as it is to assemble a peach one. As one citizen recently noted in the only *Whyville Times* article to address the subject since 2002, "I went to Akbar's and typed in Latino. I bought a head, ears and a shirt—but I was appalled at how few Latino parts there actually were. Eventually, I put together a fairly decent Latino face, even finding a Latino girly arm" (Artista 2005). The presence of accessories like a "Latino girly arm" probably represented an improvement over the past, but at least some players still were not finding it easy to complete a non-white look.

Trying on New Identities

Public discussion of race in the *Whyville Times* was not limited to discussions of available face parts. Three authors wrote articles sharing their experiences of life in Whyville with brown or olive avatars. These authors describe their interactions with other Whyvillians while they embodied their new, racialized avatars. Because these discussions deal with interactions between "real" and "virtual" identities in Gee's (2004) sense, they are a potential place to observe their authors' struggles with or reflections on the projective identities they formed while embodying particular virtual identities. Two authors who described themselves as white "in real life," Samgirl21 and Artista, decided to "experiment" by "going as" a black person and a Latina, respectively. Samgirl (2003) described her first day playing as her new black avatar in her article "Black Like Me":

Surprisingly, a girl that I vaguely knew was there and immediately approached me. "SamGirl!" she exclaimed.

"What happened?" She went on, "You look like a freak!" I was cautious and went on to ask why. She explained that being black on Whyville looks just wrong. I was appalled! I couldn't believe that this happened on my first day, my first hour of being a black Whyvillian.

Samgirl was surprised and upset by several negative experiences she had while sporting her black avatar. Early in her article, she suggested that most people, including herself, do not expect racism to be a part of the Whyville experience, writing, "You might be thinking, who's racist anymore? The Civil War is over, Martin Luther King has spoken, we're all good." However, by the end of her article, she felt she had learned something more about herself and other Whyvillians. She ended her article by encouraging other white people on Whyville to try her experiment: "Put yourself in that position. Be a minority in Whyville for a day. Be black like me." (It is notable that this suggestion demonstrates that Samgirl is writing to an assumed white audience.)

Bluegal7 (2002) wrote a similar article describing the experience of switching from "that one fashion in Whyville where all the girls had blonde hair with little extensions and white skin" to a look that was more like her own physical appearance as a self-described Latina. Her motivation to create a Latina look stemmed from imagining the intersection of her Whyville fashion habits and her "real-life" looks: "One day, I imagined if I dyed my hair blond and changed my hair color in real life just for that silly reason (fitting in) and I realized how stupid I was to change my appearance." Blue-gal7 reported feeling proud and positive after changing her looks. She did not report any of the problems that Samgirl21 and Artista reported in their "experiments" with being minority, and she does not seem to view her new look as temporary. Her article was praised in an editor's note, which the creators of Whyville occasionally use to respond to issues raised by *Times* authors.

However, not all members of the Whyville.net responded positively to articles such as "Black Like Me" and "In a Latina's Shoes." An anonymous author ("Prejudice: Not Only Race," 2003) responded doubtfully to the article, saying:

> I thought that what this girl was saying can't be true. I have a couple of friends who are black on Whyville and are very popular, one of them a very good friend of mine. I felt that Samgirl21 failed to research a bit, actually. I mean, plenty of people on Whyville who have been "black" since they started haven't gone through so many racist acts.

This argument that racism cannot be widespread because the author, a white person, has not experienced it first- or secondhand recapitulates many of the discussions on racism in the United States that have taken place among adults in nonvirtual settings. Taken together, these articles paint a picture of the kinds of experimentation with avatar race that can go on in Whyville and the community's reaction to such experimentation.

From Avatars to Friendships

In this chapter, we have focused on designing avatars as a primary form of identity play in virtual worlds. The cases we discussed in this chapter, from Zoe to Lucetta and others, demonstrate that there are many more influences on avatar design than simply one's personal desire to embody one's identity or create a new identity online. Design tools, financial resources, and perhaps most importantly social values interact with one's desires in creating avatars. Further, avatars change over time as players get to know the online world they occupy and as their expertise grows in understanding the culture, values, and tools of design in that world. Contrary to popular myth, though worlds like Whyville provide broad freedoms in making avatars, one cannot be just "anyone" online.

Further, in virtual worlds like Whyville, or other worlds where avatars have broad design freedoms, avatar parts can be a tremendous source of in-world wealth. For those who learn the digital tools to design avatar parts, creating and marketing those parts can provide a steady source of income that can rocket one to the upper echelons of virtual world society. Alternatively, if one understands fashion trends, wisely buying and trading avatar parts, as Zoe did, can provide entry into financial engagement in the virtual world. Thus avatars are not just for identity development, but also provide a prominent area of design freedom in virtual worlds that are generally made by designers for consumption by users. Becoming a designer or trader is an important form of agency that kids can develop in virtual worlds that may not be as easily accessible in other areas of their daily lives.

Our discussion of avatars and identity play provides an ideal base from which to consider the kinds of relationship play in which tweens engage in virtual worlds. Indeed, avatars are entries to relationships. If one looks like a newbie, people may ridicule or befriend one based on that assumption. If one's avatar displays expertise and wealth, people may ask to be friends, or even boyfriends and girlfriends. And if one's avatar exhibits interest in a particular hobby (like anime, horses, pets, or politics), other tweens often draw on those symbols to create a bond of common interest. Friendships can be solidified by gifting or trading avatar parts, buying jewelry for a girlfriend, or trading hair. Indeed, we often say that in Whyville one of the main goals of citizens is to earn money to build good-looking avatars in order to socialize with others—the focus of the next chapter.

4   Social Play

It is easier to ask [someone out] online because you're not really there to experience it and if you get turned down, it isn't that embarrassing, since not everyone knows and not everyone cares.

—XKaileeX[1]

I've actually been asked out by some guy who said he wanted me to be his girlfriend because I was hot. Okay, let's get this straight: you like me because my little Whyville person is HOT? I'm extremely insulted if you presume my only good quality is that the little cartoon person I use to walk around on some website is pretty.

—Aquagerl[2]

Congrats he chose u
IT'S FINE
I'M NOT JELOUS OR ANYTHING
I DON'T NEED HIM
KNO HE DOESN'T HE WANTS A NICE GURL LIK U
WE CAN TALK LIK SISTAZ
HUGZ
it doesn't matter who he wants cuz
we shouldn't hav a guy to brighten ur day
we hav each other and thats what counts

—Zoe (as bluwave, chatting with another Whyvillian)

In recent years, the role of computers in socializing has become quite prevalent,[3] and nowhere more strongly than in the lives of young people. The time we spend on the computer and online has been steadily increasing over the last two decades.[4] Virtual worlds can provide personal spaces where kids can socialize freely with peers in imaginative, fun ways. They can extend relationships with existing friends by logging in and playing from their separate homes. They can be creative—playing with different looks and imaginative tools available only in digital worlds. They can also interact with massive numbers of other kids whom they do not know from their schools or neighborhoods. And this access to other boys and girls seems to be one of the primary interests that drive interactions in Whyville.

Making social connections in a massive tween world is a challenge, and as we will see below, the relationships made online are largely cursory and short-term, often seen as collectibles as tweens chalk up how many boy-friends or girlfriends they have obtained. Yet not all connections are tran-sient. Tweens also use online spaces to extend existing relationships and to make new ones based on common interests. Even when relationships are more casual, from a developmental standpoint this is not always a nega-tive thing. In this chapter, we outline some of the challenges that shape tweens' social play in virtual worlds. We then dive into the social play in the after-school club, play that stretched across the settings of the club, school, and Whyville. We do this by investigating the dynamics surrounding the practice of throwing projectiles—a socially interactive activity that wove together connections in the club and helped establish new relationships online. Next, we turn to the topic of romance, taking a broad look at how tweens view romantic relationships in Whyville and what they actually do. Finally, we consider the delicate issue of tweens' capability to be responsible when social boundaries are crossed inappropriately in a virtual world, and how club members responded to a particular incident of this nature.

Hanging Out Online

Hanging out is one of the most basic ways kids engage with each other, especially as they move into adolescence, but it can be also a precursor to deeper involvement in "messing around" or "geeking out" with digital media.[5] One of the primary reasons for hanging out with peers is that it is an important part of young people's social development. Indeed, Sub-rahmanyam, Greenfield, and Tynes[6] found that teens and young adults tackle many of the traditional developmental tasks, like exploring romantic relationships, online as well as offline, albeit with some important differ-ences. Anonymity and the invisibility of physical bodies allowed youth in their study, especially girls, to be freer in what they said and to whom they said it, as well as in their exploration of gendered and sexualized identities. One would expect to see similar types of explorations among younger youth, especially tweens. Research on tweens' socializing in general points to "anticipatory socialization,"[7] or perhaps more to the point, "anticipatory enculturation,"[8] the ways that young people look forward to being more like those older than themselves. Tweens anticipate the kinds of things they will do when they are a little older, such as dressing more maturely, enjoying "teen" music or books, and flirting. Because bodies and ages are anonymous in virtual worlds, they provide a prime avenue from which to pursue these anticipatory practices.

Socializing in virtual worlds can serve to promote connections with people kids already know, to develop relationships with new people in a massive populated environment, and to move across these "known" and "unknown" individuals. Granovetter's[9] classic work in sociology points to dual human needs to develop "strong ties" with a few close friends and family as well as "weak ties" with many other individuals. There is strong evidence that participation in online social worlds helps teens and young adults strengthen existing relationships by providing another environment in which to continue relationships from home, school, neighborhood, or elsewhere.[10] This can be particularly important for kids whose families are distributed throughout the world, like migrant youth or kids who have immigrated.[11] In some situations, kids use online sites not only to keep up relationships with friends and family who have moved away, but also to deepen their knowledge of their native languages, history, or culture.[12]

Online social worlds are also known to promote weak ties—relationships with people one knows but may not be in a close relationship with. For instance, one study demonstrated that youth with low self-esteem were able to use Facebook to follow news and gossip in their high schools, even though they were not in the "in" crowd.[13] In other words, Facebook provided a way for teens to strengthen "weak ties" with people they knew but were not close with in ways that promoted their confidence about knowing what was happening with people at school. There is also evidence that having a large number of weak ties can provide kids with opportunities to get to know others with different backgrounds. Through this they can take on the perspectives of others, for instance those of a race or ethnicity different from themselves. Tynes[14] argues that interacting with others about these topics online can alleviate some of the social and emotional concerns that are often present in face-to-face interactions with others of different backgrounds. Yet she also found that negative stereotypes and racial prejudice persist online alongside these more positive opportunities, a finding not dissimilar to our own research in Whyville regarding race and avatar design (see chapter 3).

With this background on strong and weak ties, exploration of new relationships in low-risk online settings, and developmental needs to explore romance and anticipate new types of relationships coming up in the teenage years, let us dig deeper into social play in Whyville. We begin by journeying into tweens' relationships with each other in the club and exploring how their social play extended across spaces available to them at school, the club, and on Whyville before considering how their play then reached out to the broader social world of Whyvillians at large. We do this through an investigation of projectile throwing—a predominantly social activity that became common practice among nearly all members of the after-school club and revealed their connected play with each other.

Projectile Throwing as Connected Play

Projectile throwing[15] is a common practice on Whyville akin to snowball fights, pulling a girl's pigtails, and playing catch. All one had to do was purchase some projectiles, take aim, and throw. The projectile would appear beside one's own avatar and travel in a straight line to the person aimed at, stick to him or her (if it was well aimed) for a couple of seconds, and then disappear. If it was a certain type of projectile, like a Frisbee or a football, it would emerge in the recipient's inventory and she could throw it back in a game of catch.[16] In Whyville, projectile throwing is a way to "reach out and touch someone," a playful way of making connections with others.

Of course, this all depends on which projectile one throws. Throwing a ball is one thing, and generally players intended balls to be thrown back. Briana was a particular fan of throwing balls and Frisbees with friends in the club as a form of play on Whyville and also to make friends with other Whyvillians. In fact, her first throw was a football to some Whyvillians she didn't know from school. The fun of throwing a Frisbee back and forth caught on with some other girls from the club as well. One evening when Leslie and Marissa were together on Whyville they met on Saturn. The following conversation ensued, where Leslie (peachy5) threw a purple Frisbee ("Pfrisbee") at Marissa (lucky7) and explained to her how to throw it back.

Leslie/Peachy5	19:34:13	Throw Pfrisbee lucky7
Marissa/lucky7	19:34:22	Ydouwant2throwafrisbyatme?
Leslie/Peachy5	19:34:37	So u can trow it back
Marissa/lucky7	19:35:11	Achooy
Leslie/Peachy5	19:35:18	Say "trow Pfrisbee Peachy5"
Leslie/Peachy5	19:35:46	Hello r u there
Marissa/lucky7	19:35:52	Yea
Marissa/lucky7	19:36:07	I just keep on sneazing
Leslie/Peachy5	19:36:33	Say "throw Pfrisbee Peachy5"
Leslie/Peachy5	19:37:13	O well
Marissa/lucky7	19:37:24	Throw pfrisbee Peachy5
Leslie/Peachy5	19:37:37	Yay!!!!!!

Meeting together on Whyville outside of the club and in separate locations, Leslie and Marissa enjoyed throwing the Frisbee as a way to play with each other, creating an interactive, collaborative activity that in one sense is exemplary of connected play, especially as it connected them across a distance, as they played from their own homes.

In contrast, most of the boys in the club threw projectiles to create a type of war game, utilizing snowballs, mudballs, and maggots in this endeavor. Aidan often called out, "Meet me at the Pool!" and several boys would dash to the Whyville Pool where one of them would throw a mudball at another. The others would retaliate and a projectile war would ensue, with laughter and exclamations from all parties. Sometimes this mudball fight in Whyville would carry over into the club with a light-hearted roughhousing, as someone just hit with a mudball would leave his computer, run to the perpetrator's seat, and wrestle with the offending club member. It was quite common for club members to run from computer to computer to see what each person was doing and to give a running commentary on the activity about who had hit whom and what that person did in return (often cheering one another to hit back).

This play between club members frequently involved inadvertent Whyvillians as well, especially when someone missed a target. One day when Blake decided to take aim at his fellow club members, he said with suspense in his voice, "I wanna throw at Gabe, at Gabe!" Blake aimed and threw, but his pie missed Gabe and hit a girl instead. Watching this event, Scott jumped up from his computer to tell Gabe, "He threw it at you but he missed, he missed." Hitting an innocent Whyvillian simply increased the fun of the game.

As the club progressed, members began to use projectiles to interact with Whyvillians at large with a variety of motivations. The boys began to throw projectiles at Whyville girls as part of flirting: "I threw a heart at my girlfriend." They would also throw things at various Whyvillians for a number of reasons that seemed to set them apart from themselves. They would throw at people who looked different, stood out, or looked odd: "Throw it at that guy, since he thinks he's so cool," "Let's get the carrot dude," "Hey, Goth is ugly." When asked by one of the researchers, "Why do you throw a projectile at someone?" Aidan replied, "Cause you don't like them." The researcher pressed further, "Would you throw it at a friend for fun?" and Aidan responded, "Yeah, that's what I do to Blake all the time." So there were multiple reasons for throwing projectiles—as part of collaborative play with known friends, to set people apart (as members of the opposite sex, ugly, or just different), and even to flirt. Occasionally, a boy would tell someone not to throw anything at him, but more often they vied for each other's attention when they successfully hit others with various projectiles: "Guys, go to the pool party, I threw a spider at her!" A particularly successful way to get attention was to throw a heart at another boy in the club, drawing on gendered and romantic connotations of heart symbols and generally breaking down in giggles as a result. These kinds of play reflect Barrie Thorne's concept of "borderwork" that produces sexual and romantic meanings in play with peers while also recoiling from physical proximity.[17] Projectile throwing allows for touching at a distance, creating symbolic connections while still being able to giggle about the borders crossed in doing so.

The Hidden Play of Girls: Flirting

While projectile throwing was an obvious form of play for the boys of the club who did it very publicly, it was less obvious for the girls. Few girls seemed to engage in projectile throwing during the club, and those that did only appeared to do it for fun with other members. Yet when we began looking at logfiles that recorded what players did on Whyville, we realized that not only were girls like Briana and Zoe some of the most frequent projectile throwers in the club, but several girls also used projectiles in flirting, an activity that went unnoticed by us until we studied their online logs. This is because while the boys advertised their flirting loudly, bragging about their pickup lines and broadcasting times when they threw things at girls, the girls kept these practices to themselves.

The case of Isabel's learning how to throw projectiles provides a pertinent example of how figuring out how to throw a projectile at another club member could be quickly applied as a form of flirtatious play. One day several weeks into the after-school club, Isabel and Cole were sitting next to each other at neighboring computers. Cole yelled in a loud voice to the club at large, "Okay you guys, meet me at the Beach, no, at the Pool Party!" Having issued his invitation to meet at a specific place in Whyville (the Pool Party), he then went to the Projectile Shoppe to stock up on projectiles to throw at any club members who met him at the Pool Party (see figure 4.1). From Cole's activity, it is clear that he intentionally stocked up a number of projectiles for every eventuality, from throwing at friends to flirting with his girlfriend (e.g., throwing flowers or kisses).

From the very beginning, Isabel showed interest in Cole's club-wide invitation to meet at the Pool Party, but while Cole was shopping her curiosity peaked and she began making suggestions for what he should buy as well as expressing wonderment about the various types of projectiles for sale: "Mudball, Red Paintball, Chocolate?" Obviously, one cannot throw projectiles without buying them, and her observation and semiparticipation in Cole's shopping spree appear to have both sparked her interest and provided her with the needed exposure to the Projectile Shoppe to buy her own projectiles several minutes later.

Sometime between Cole's shopping and her own shopping, Isabel joined Cole and others at the Pool Party. While there she learned how to identify Cole by his looks on Whyville (it is always a bit tricky to recognize your friends in a crowded room of avatars). After watching Cole throw at a few people Isabel declared, "Okay, I want to get something," and went straight to the Projectile Shoppe, this time to shop for herself. Upon returning from the Shoppe, Isabel solicited Cole's help in correctly spelling "throw" and looked at his screen as he typed in his own command to throw a projectile. He also helped her to spell Zoe's username (bluwave) since he was instructing her to throw at Zoe and engage her in their playful war. Their physical proximity made it easier for Isabel to learn how to engage in this particular kind of social play.

Perhaps most intriguing is what happened after Isabel finally learned how to throw a projectile. With projectiles in hand and some knowledge

Cole:	[Cole loudly invites people to meet at Pool Party]	Cole shops for projectiles, listing different kinds for different purposes.
Isabel:	Four pies, four mudballs, four—No wait, go down? No get, um, [pointing at projectiles on the screen]	
Cole:	I need to get one pair of flowers for my girlfriend, a kiss for my girlfriend.	
Isabel:	Oh I already have some hearts.Purple paintball, mudball, red paintball. Chocolate?	Isabel explores available projectiles
…	…	…
Isabel:	Wait where are you?	Isabel figures out what Cole looks like on Whyville, identifying him in the crowd.
Cole:	I don't know.	
Isabel:	Oh you're right there.	
Cole:	I splatted the person behind you. I tried to splat you but I splatted the person behind you. "Throw pie" [typing] Webster where are you? "Yoda" [typing Webster's username] Webster—go inside the mall to the food court!	Cole throws something at Isabel but misses.
Isabel:	Okay I want to get something.	After watching the projectile battle, Isabel decides to get some projectiles of her own.
…	[Isabel goes to Projectile Shoppe]	…
Isabel:	Oh oh, I want—I want to throw a projectile. That guy's freaky looking. How you spell throw again? T-h-[looking over at Finn's screen] T-h-r. [goes to her own screen]	Later, after watching Cole throw more projectiles at club members, Isabel decides to throw herself. She asks for help on Mechanics of throwing.
…	…	…
Cole:	Yes come on help me throw projectiles at Zoe [bluwave].	Cole invites Isabel into the projectile-throwing war in the club.
Isabel:	[typing] I'm throwing it at this—	
Cole:	Oh man he's not there anymore.	

Isabel:	Oh I hit someone in front of you!	
Cole:	Yeah. [giggles]	
Isabel:	Who am I supposed to be throwing this at?	Isabel asks for Social instruction on whom to throw at.
Cole:	Boom. Pied you with your own pie. Bluwave, okay?	Cole tells her to throw at a club member and gives her username.
Isabel:	Okay. Well no wait. What's her name?	
Cole:	Bluwave.	
Isabel:	No I'm doing this at somebody else.	Isabel determines to do her own thing.
Isabel:		Types "throw a mud ball at sunboy90"

Figure 4.1
Isabel learns to throw a projectile.

of how to throw them, Isabel faced the task of deciding who her target should be. Although Cole directed her to throw at Zoe, Isabel changed her mind and decided, "No I'm doing this at somebody else." So who did she throw at? For her target, Isabel elected to throw a mudball at a Whyvillian boy: "throw a mud ball at sunboy90." This particular attempt did not succeed because she typed the command incorrectly, but later she frequently engaged in throwing projectiles at many Whyville boys, taking up flirtatious play that was hidden from her peers at the club. Eventually Isabel's projectile throwing moved across several different planes of social play, from playing with club members as she had with Cole, to flirtatious throwing at boys in Whyville, to further throwing at club members when the club was over, meeting friends online and throwing at them.

Several other girls in the club also flirted regularly, both with projectiles and with other forms of flirting. The projectile throwing by Isabel was part of a long trajectory of flirting with Whyvillians as one of her primary activities. She was often on the lookout for potential boyfriends. Briana also flirted with many people on Whyville for her first few weeks, though she commented in the club that, "Whydating is whack" and "I just think it's funny." That these girls' flirting was hidden in the club suggests that the anonymity available in Whyville did indeed provide them with social freedom to play with their gendered and sexual identities.[18] Below we delve deeper into the practices of flirting on Whyville and the ways that they were often anticipatory in nature.

Valentine Games: Exploring Romance in Whyville

On January 15, her fifth day in Whyville, new phrases began appearing in Zoe's chat: "r u single" and "wanna hook up?" Later on other lines popped up: "a/s/l" (an abbreviated way to ask about someone's age, sex, and location) and "u r hot." Zoe had begun the nearly ubiquitous practice of flirting in Whyville. At first this flirting merely imitated phrases that were commonly used in crowded places in the virtual world. But she quickly grew more sophisticated, and only a few days later she told some classmates on Whyville that "I almost have a boyfriend … because he told me to y-mail him … all he has to do." Zoe was bragging about securing an official boyfriend in Whyville, something generally seen as an accomplishment in that massive world. They had conversed and he had asked her to ymail him, which she had. All he had to do was ymail back and the relationship, such as it was, would be sealed.

Though this early flirting was highly imitational, Zoe became more original and selective in flirting over the months she inhabited Whyville, picking and choosing what she said with particular purposes in mind. For instance, several weeks into her membership, she began playing with her age as a way to encourage or discourage potential suitors based on her impressions of them. If she wanted to turn away someone who was flirting with her she might tell the truth about her age—"im way too young 4 u … i'm just 12" (February 1)—while if she wanted to encourage a flirtation, she would lie about her age, claiming she was thirteen years old and living in Los Angeles. One of these encounters is quoted below (February 13):

do u think i'm hot???

13. /f/la

…

r we bf and gf?

kk

whymail me

Here Zoe solicited flirtation by commenting on her looks ("do u think i'm hot???") then gave her age/sex/location as 13/female/Los Angeles, adding a year to her actual age. Finally she confirmed that they were boyfriend and girlfriend ("bf and gf") and asked her new boyfriend to ymail her, verifying the new status of their relationship. These sorts of conversations happened regularly through the course of her second and third months on Whyville. Then her flirting became less frequent. Instead of the short conversations to get a boyfriend, she invested conversational effort in friendships that lasted longer, and her occasional flirtations changed from the simple solicitation-confirmation-ymail pattern (described above) to longer conversations with what appear to be the same individuals rather than new ones each time.

Romantic Play in Whyville

All of these interactions are typical of the casual flirtation that takes place frequently on Whyville.[19] Zoe's adoption of these practices could be considered a sign that she was trying out some of the ways that Whyvillians interact. Yet though she started out simply imitating what she saw in others' chat, she adapted these practices as she became more familiar with Whyville, and later altered them altogether, as she largely dropped out of flirting and began to develop what appear to be more extended friendships. Flirting is a common practice on Whyville. The age group that participates on Whyville (eight to sixteen years old) may have something to do with the frequency of flirting, as youth this age tend to engage in "anticipatory socialization,"[20] imitating the flirting practices that they observe in older youth and on popular media. Indeed, Barrie Thorne and Valerie Walkerdine have both described how much bodies and sexuality take center stage in children's everyday interactions on playgrounds and in whispered conversation in school.[21] Children on the cusp of adolescence ponder, imagine, and imitate what will happen as they develop and reach the ages of their friends and siblings who are just a few years older. As we investigated flirting in Whyville, we documented practices that indeed fit with this anticipatory model of flirting, albeit adapted for a virtual environment.

Most flirting involved casual ways of finding potential members of the opposite sex in crowded, populous areas in Whyville. One popular form of doing this was by spamming phrases like "r u single" or "123 if ur single." Interested individuals would respond with "123" if they were single and interested. Other forms of the initial solicitation included "555 if im hot" or

"654 if im cute," allowing others to respond in kind. Of course, as Aquagerl said in her article quoted at the beginning of this chapter, what "hot" meant on Whyville was solely a response to one's two-dimensional avatar, and not everyone was pleased by this form of flirtation: "I'm extremely insulted if you presume my only good quality is that the little cartoon person I use to walk around on some website is pretty." Another common flirtation practice was using the abbreviation found in singles ads or in online chat rooms: a/s/l, for age/sex/location. A player would ask "a/s/l" of people she was interested in and they would respond by giving their age, gender, and general location, for example: "12/F/LA" for twelve years old, female, from Los Angeles, or "13/M/USA" for thirteen years old, male, from the United States. Of course there was no way to tell whether a person was telling the truth or not, and most of the tweens we studied lied frequently about their age, either inflating it for people they were interested in (pretending they were teenagers) or deflating it for those they were not interested in (pretending they were younger in order to dissuade others). This shows that tweens were quite comfortable choosing which information to share and using it to shape what kind of interactions they wanted to have. Lying about one's age also reflects the anticipatory nature of this social play of flirting, pretending to be older in order to "date" others in Whyville.

On most occasions, flirtations never went past this initial spamming of pickup lines or exchanges of a/s/l, but every now and then a couple would follow up on a flirtation. There were several ways to follow up a relationship in Whyville, and almost all of them involved relocation to a more private space, getting away from the crowd to relatively secluded locations like Saturn, the Moon, or Mars. Even though maintaining a private conversation was easily possible in a public area through whispering (privately chatting person to person), moving to a new place where couples could be alone was still preferred. Once alone, couples might chat about their shared interests or simply get straight to the point by saying, "I love you" or "I really like you." A projectile might be thrown: a heart, kiss, or flowers. Sometimes one person would ask, "r we bf/gf" in an attempt to confirm the status of a relationship as boyfriend/girlfriend. Often within just a few minutes of chatting, the couple might promise to ymail and go their separate ways. Or one person might send a face part to another, such as a necklace or piece of jewelry. Cole in fact bragged that he had twenty girlfriends and that it was difficult to keep them stocked up on gifts. Another boy from the club said that having a girlfriend on Whyville meant that "You give them stuff." In many ways such as this, romance in Whyville was commodified: exchanging gifts, bribing with clams, and collecting boyfriends and girlfriends. This commodification of romance seems to have continued on Whyville, although with a shift toward girls gifting clams to boys to be their boyfriends, as several of our 2008 club members experienced. Usually, relationships never left this casual existence of exchanging ymails, conversations, and gifts.

On rarer occasions couples sought out closer contact by "touching" in the virtual space. Whyville's version of physical contact is for two avatars to stand overlapping each other, akin to cuddling or holding hands, or sometimes perceived as kissing or making out ("m/o"). Sometimes discussions would arise about making out, but Whyvillians as a whole did not tend to role play in this way. Coordinated dancing was also a way for avatars to "touch" each other, a stronger statement of intimacy sometimes perceived as sexual play. A simple dance where two avatars moved up and down with a slight bounce in synchronized motion was one way to accomplish this. Interestingly enough, dancing is somewhat difficult on Whyville. Both avatars must say "dance bop" or a similar dance at the same time for them to bounce in sync with each other. Whyvillians can create their own dances by going to the dance studio and using graphing on an x-y axis and timing in order to create a series of steps where the avatar moves from one x-y coordinate to another with specific timing. In some ways, being intimate on Whyville could be a very complicated procedure.

Whyville Times Writers on Romantic Play

Even if flirting is a common practice in Whyville, this does not mean that all citizens agree with it. In fact, Whyvillians expressed a wide range of views on romance in Whyville, or "Whydating" as some called it.[22] In general, *Whyville Times* writers recognized that dating in Whyville was highly popular, and a few authors supported it without question. However, most authors qualified their support or criticized the practice wholesale, from casual flirtations to more serious romantic encounters to "Whymarriage" and "Whybabies."[23] Many writers commented with distaste on the ubiquitous practice of flirting in Whyville. For instance, in an article entitled "Behind the Veil," authors Liss22 and Piker outlined what they perceived as a typical flirtation:

Lots of people on Whyville are going out with someone. Or with someone's friend, or a friend of a friend. ... If you're not sure how it goes, the typical conversation is like this:

Piker: Hey.
Liss22:   Hey.
Piker: You're cute. =)
Liss22:   So are you!
Piker: Single?
Liss22:   Why? =)
Piker: Wanta go out?

You might be thinking, *"Yeah right, it's not like that!!,"* but it is! Maybe it's not so common with the older citizens, who will find out stuff like first name, age, favorite sport or food, how long they've been on Whyville or who they are friends with. But when the younger people start to mimic this whole "going out" thing, it turns out like what happened above. No joke. And it affects all types of people, whether they are newbies or oldies, young or old, rich or poor, pretty or unattractive. Same as real life.[24]

One complaint issued by Liss22 and Piker was that kids did not get to know one another before beginning to date; whereas "older citizens" might find out more about a person, most people only had a simple conversation before deciding to go out. This was a common objection to dating in the *Whyville Times*. Mikay37 observed that "people are looking for a b/f or g/f in any way they can. They'll ask right out if you're single or not."[25] She went on to describe how one could never be sure who was on the other end of the flirtation, that one could have no idea of whether that person was actually "hot" or not or even how old they were. This echoes Aquagerl's concern quoted at the beginning of this chapter that people wanted to date her simply because they thought her avatar looked cool: "I'm extremely insulted if you presume my only good quality is that the little cartoon person I use to walk around on some website is pretty."

A number of *Whyville Times* reporters, male and female, also expressed frustration at being constantly "hit on" with questions like, "Do you have a gf?" or "Are you single?"[26] For some, this spamming of pickup lines was simply annoying, while for others, some flirting was offensive enough to merit a 911 report, such as when a guy asked Holiday50 if he could "eat [her] donuts," where "'donuts' was merely a clever synonym for [her] breasts."[27] In this case, flirting did cross the line between appropriate and inappropriate behavior, as an explicit sexual reference was made.

Despite this, Holiday50 and a few other *Times* writers still argued for a nuanced stance toward flirting, arguing that flirtatious behavior was okay as long as you would engage in the same behavior in real life: "Mild flirting but still quite casual. In real life if a man were to say to me what this boy said, my remark would be the same."[28] Several authors discussed Whydating as positive when individuals engaged in age-appropriate behaviors and remained conscious of the dangers of online dating. For example, in an early advertisement for the Love and Dating Club (LADC), Lilly2000 emphasized the club's supportive role in "help[ing] girls and guys deal with asking out, flirting, and dating,"[29] and many of her interviewees cited the chance to try dating in a virtual environment as a lower-risk alternative to real-life dating. Some took it so far as to engage in "Whymarriage," although there were a number of reasons for this, among them popularity and profit. Indeed, Punkst3r[30] supported Whymarriage primarily because he owned a "church" where people had to pay to hold their ceremonies. In contrast, others opposed Whymarriage because it wasn't taken seriously and because they imagined it might lead to cybersex or other practices forbidden by Whyville officials and by values external to Whyville.

Times writers often responded to the practices of flirting with some concern and used their articles to reach out to these Whyvillians. Interestingly enough, many authors were savvy enough to recognize that flirting and dating on Whyville was anticipatory, imitating older kids' (teenagers) dating without forming actual romantic relationships. For instance, xXOscarXx noted with shock that she had seen kids aged nine and ten years old asking people out, commenting that "they are only doing this to 'be cool.'"[31] Like xXOscarXx, JasmineK expressed unease that younger kids on Whyville "should not be dating, least of all someone they don't know" and advised these individuals that they would "all have plenty of wonderful, meaningful real-life relationships—when [they're] ready."[32] Casc302 interviewed three middle- and high-school aged individuals and concluded in her article that dating was a developmentally appropriate behavior that tweens and teens should engage in when they are individually ready for it and have parental approval.[33] Although *Whyville Times* writers are not parents, developmental psychologists, or educators, their writings express reflective viewpoints on flirting in a virtual world, suggesting that tweens are capable of considering their own behavior and the behaviors of others and discussing the appropriateness of it. How interesting to see tween authors cautioning against behaviors they saw as developmentally inappropriate for children!

A survey that we conducted in 2009 suggests that dating is not as frequent as one might suppose and that many tweens discuss virtual dating with their parents.[34] Only 21 percent of Whyvillians who responded to our survey claimed to have a girlfriend or boyfriend online, and of those, half said that their parents knew about it. This leaves only a small 10 percent of responding tweens who had an online girlfriend or boyfriend who did not talk with their parents about it. In contrast, more tweens (35 percent) claimed they had a girlfriend or boyfriend in real life. Although flirting may be a common practice in Whyville, having a virtual boyfriend or girlfriend is less common than having one you know face to face.

Interestingly, we found no significant differences between girls and boys or by age in Whyville, except that boys thought it was significantly more important to have a boyfriend or girlfriend than girls did.[35] Tweens also predominantly sought information about dating from friends of the same gender, whether face to face or virtually in Whyville. This prioritization of peers of the same gender as a primary source of information is consistent with prior research on gender and friendships.[36] Next to friends of the same gender, popular media like TV shows and movies were also a primary source of information on dating, more than parents or even the Internet. This phenomenon is not unknown, though many may find it troubling that the popular media is such a common place to get information about dating and romance.[37] However, more encouraging is that nearly half of the tweens surveyed said that they got their information from multiple sources.

In discussing flirting and sharing our findings based on observations, interviews, surveys, and the writings of Whyville tweens themselves, we have found that flirting is a common practice in Whyville and that it is a common developmental feature of tweens' activity in general, whether in person or online. This is not to say that there is no reason for concern over tweens flirting in virtual worlds like Whyville; but most activities associated with flirting are playful and casual explorations. Of course, at times some Whyvillians cross the line and move into areas that are sexually inappropriate. But in general, based on our observations of tweens' flirting and the articles by the *Times* authors, most tweens seem to know when this line is crossed and how to respond. Below we share a specific example of this when club members dealt with a stranger who crossed boundaries in flirting with one of the members. This "incident" brings us back full circle to where we began this chapter with discussions of tweens socializing both with friends they knew in person (such as in school) and with people they knew only virtually in Whyville. The example also demonstrates one way that connected play—between school friends in a club and a virtual world, with helpful adults present—can be safe play.

The Incident: When Social Boundaries Are Crossed

About six weeks into the after-school gaming club, thirteen students and one adult clustered around the classroom's ten computers. Conversation in the club centered on the usual topics: club members compared their salaries, discussed game-playing strategies, and gave one another fashion advice on the styles available at Akbar's Face Mall. Within Whyville, they spent time socializing with their friends, communicating via ymail, "throwing" projectiles at one another, and "teleporting" to various locations. The conversations taking place in the after-school club overlapped with one another as the individuals physically present in the room also interacted with one another online.

Ulani and Blake were arranging to chat on Mars when Ulani loudly announced to everyone present that someone was asking her "something weird" on Saturn. She then clarified, "They're saying, 'wanna *do it* with me?'" Immediately Blake ran from his chair across the room to the computer where Ulani was playing. The adult present was already discussing the situation with Ulani, who announced that she would file a 911 report to document the other individual's inappropriate behavior to the Whyville authorities. Other members of the after-school club announced their presence on Saturn or made their way there as the situation gained momentum. Blake announced that he wanted to "go to Saturn and see the evidence" and suggested that everyone in the club should file a 911 report. Then Blake teleported to Saturn.

From this moment on, Blake took on a leadership role as a team of players pursued the offending individual. Soon Aidan, Marissa, and Cory were also involved. Aidan announced that he would "get something on this guy," and Blake responded, "Yeah, get someone on him" and began to organize the purchase of projectiles to throw at the objectionable individual. While Blake, Aidan, and Cory debated what type of projectiles they should purchase, Blake made his way back to the computer he was sharing with Cory and announced, "To the rescue!" to the entire room before focusing his attention on Ulani's Whyville avatar, Violet. In the meantime, Aidan located the offensive individual, threw a projectile, and announced, "Violet! ... I got him for you." In the club, Ulani thanked Aidan and worried that the offensive individual would retaliate, even as Blake pelted him with more pie projectiles. Upon a successful pie throw, Blake did a victory dance in the club and then high-fived several of his friends both online and in the club.

As the retaliative effort continued, even more club members became involved in throwing projectiles at the perpetrator and calling him names. Once most of the members were on Saturn, they lined up their avatars and counted down before engaging in a collective pie-throwing effort. Then, as they attempted to organize another round of projectile throwing, this time with the addition of "mudballs," the offender fled Saturn. Aidan and Blake immediately volunteered to "go patrol the area." When other members joined in, they split up and visited other public rooms such as Sector Y, the bazaar, the beach, the mall, and the food court looking for the offensive individual. Marissa eventually found him at the beach, but he disappeared into the crowd before the club members were able to take action. They then debated looking him up in city records, filing another 911 report, or going off to play checkers. The incident had drawn to a close.

Their time in the after-school club was also drawing to a close, and the adult present asked them to log out of Whyville and prepare to go home. As the club session wound down, members shifted their attention to other topics. But first thing the following day at the club, Blake received a ymail stating that the offending person had been banned from Whyville.

"The incident," as we have come to call it, was perhaps one of the most connected events that occurred in the club. The entire club engaged in synchronized activity on- and off-Whyville focused on retaliating against an individual who had said something very inappropriate to one of their own. It catapulted many members to learn how to teleport and throw projectiles[38] for the first time. More importantly, the tween club members handled the situation well. Ulani reported what was said to her to the club, an adult present helped direct her to filing a "911 report" in Whyville, and the members at large recognized that the statement, "wanna do it with me," was beyond the boundaries of appropriate behavior in a virtual world like Whyville. Our observations of the incident do not suggest that tweens should be left to deal with such issues on their own. However, given the appropriate support (a supervising adult in the classroom, parents, a 911 reporting tool), tweens may surprise us with what they are capable of handling.

We view this as a first step toward better understanding the potential of engaging tweens in self-governance in virtual worlds. Everyone in the club had passed a "chat test," which provided information on the difference between simply annoying and actually inappropriate chat. All members had been informed by Whyville of what to do in both cases, and in this situation members responded appropriately. They also rallied around each other enthusiastically. Although we do not know if tweens playing together online but not physically present in the same room would always respond in the same way, the supportive environment of the after-school club assisted with the tweens' collective response. It suggests that tweens *can* handle some self-governance in a virtual world, with appropriate preparation and training on taking up the responsibilities of play. Connected play with face-to-face and virtual friends in a virtual world may provide a safer environment for facing such issues than simply one environment alone. Many long-time members of Whyville already serve in leadership capacities: ymail helpers, tour guides, elected "Senate" members, even *Whyville Times* reporters. We hope that other researchers will continue to explore the issue of governance in adult-, teen-, and child-focused virtual worlds, taking into account the specific needs and interests of each population.

In this chapter, we have considered various aspects of tweens' social play in Whyville: learning and playing with each other, imitating social practices like flirting, anticipating ways that older kids act, and eventually adapting their own styles of socializing in a massive world with both known and new friends. In the end, club members demonstrated the ability to attend responsibly to a challenging situation when a Whyvillian crossed a boundary from appropriate to inappropriate social interaction. In the next chapter, we consider play on the edges of other boundaries—those between virtual settings and concerning values of right and wrong in virtual worlds.

5 Boundary Play

Hey! this is Rj coming to ya with another (yes, I know, another) scandal! Listen to this one: I was in Whyville square today and I saw a kinda sorta almost newbie (she didn't have the newbie face, but she had cheap clothes). She was asking people how to make more clams. She said she had a low salary and needed more. So, me being me, I said, go to the Sun Spot, play the alien game, go to the Illision House, sign up for smart cars, and try the Rocket design at WASA. (Can't you just feel a BUT coming …?) BUT … two girls responded differently! These two girls said, "Go to GRAND-MA'S and get some face parts. Then sell 'em!!" OMGosh! You do NOT go to Grandma's to get rich! NO NO NO! You go to Grandma's when you're a newbie and you truly need some face parts! I am very upset! When I heard what they said, I went nuts! I didn't curse or anything, I just went NUTS! (Go ahead, ask them!) How can you do that? People donate to Grandma's expecting to help newbies, not help a rich person get richer! Your not only ripping off the donors, you're jacking the newbies too! Now I was mad at first, but then I was hurt. How can you people do that? The CW (City Workers) and the 'Dudes' (my word for the people you don't see on Whyville. The people working at the computers 24/7) made Grandma for you! And you're ripping her off.

This is RJ signing off, very ashamed.

—RJ[1]

Most of the daily activities of thousands of players in Whyville are quite mundane—playing science games, checking banking accounts, adjusting avatar looks, hanging out with others—and not much to worry about. Occasionally though, we get a glimpse of other activities that are more questionable, particularly those that involve scamming and cheating others. The observation above by RJ, a Whyville player, about ripping off Grandma's by selling face parts to make clams, sits on a thin line dividing the acceptable from the questionable. Lying, cheating, and scamming—all boundary play is a matter of heated debate as well as actual concern for all kids, both online and offline. Play with peers is about establishing and negotiating values, what counts as right and wrong. Deciding how values from home, school, and other areas fit into relations in a new environment, virtual worlds, is at the core of online play. It is a territory for rich deliberation, since what is considered questionable in one context may be common practice in another. When is it okay to cheat in science games? When should one circumnavigate chat filters? When are actions simply playful and when do they cross the line and begin hurting others? For Zoe and many others, boundary play became a particular matter of concern when sometimes as victims, sometimes as perpetrators, they became involved in scams.

On February 21, six weeks into her life in Whyville, Zoe began using the Trading Post in a new way—to scam or defraud other Whyvillians out of their clams.[2] It began when she herself was scammed. In the main lobby of the Trading Post, where Whyvillians mill around trying to identify people to trade with before moving on to a specific Trade Room, some Whyvillians were broadly soliciting people who wanted their "clams doubled." Zoe expressed interest in this and followed them to the designated Trade Room (#48), but on finding out the details she expressed skepticism:

2:53 p.m.	Trade Room 48
	O SRRY
2:54 p.m.	i don't beleive u!!!!
	WAIT
	r u just gonnin on his side>>>>>
2:55 p.m.	fine
	r u a scammer?? TELL THE TRUTH
2:56 p.m.	fine ill do it
	get back in the chair ill do it
	soo what am i supposed 2 do?

After pressing the soliciting Whyvillians, "r u a scammer?? TELL THE TRUTH," she agreed to their methods, which consisted of one person (Zoe, the victim) putting all her clams up in a one-sided trade while the others put nothing up for trade. After the other party left their seat (giving the illusion of the trade ending), Zoe was told to press "agree" to complete the trade, thus giving all of her clams to the scammers.

Once the trade had been completed, Zoe left the room and checked her bank statement only to realize that all of her clams were gone. Then she went immediately back to the Trading Post where she begged time and again for people to donate five clams to her (the amount charged for each trade)—she was so bereft that she could not even trade face parts! She tracked down the culprits who tricked her, confronted them, and briefly followed them to their Trade Room to try to stop the next victim from falling prey to their scam. The "<<<<" in the conversation below were used to point directly at the culprit. Zoe most likely went to the right of the culprit and used the arrows to point left at the culprit, then moved to the other side and pointed again at the culprit.

3:13 p.m.	Trading Post Lobby
	U GUYS SCAMMED ME!!!!!!!!!
3:14 p.m.	Trade Room 1
	y did u scam me??
3:15 p.m.	Trade Room 48
	<<<<don't do it shes a scammer
3:16 p.m.	i did it and i got my clamz scammed>>>>

Shortly after this she gave up on trying to disrupt their scam; and, after finally succeeding in getting someone to give her five clams, she began attempting the same scam on others.

Over the next two weeks, Zoe consistently tried to get unsuspecting Whyvillians to fall for the "clam doubling" scam, as it is known among Whyville designers. This involved going to densely populated areas in Whyville like the City Beach and the Trading Post Lobby and asking people, "do u want ur clamz doubled?" If someone expressed interest, she directed him to a specific trading room and told him, "put up all of ur clamz plz," and then instructed him, "ok when i get out of the chair press the agree." From a chat frequency count, we know that she used the word "doubled" over 200 times, demonstrating persistency and intensity in her scamming activity, as it did not continue past two weeks. In a single day (February 25), she actually recruited for her scam thirty times in ninety minutes and got six people to go to a trading room. We know that she completed her scam at least once and probably enough times to keep her continuing at it for a time. Below is an account of when she successfully completed her scam:

11:44 am	The Moon
	do u want ur clamz doubled?
11:45 am	rm 49 at the trading post kk
	Foyer, Trade Room 49
	…
	put up ur clamz plz
11:48 am	ok when i get out of the chair press agree the typ
	all clear?
11:49 am	leave
	Index, tradeResult, oneMail, delete, records, userDetails
11:50 am	records, userDetails, index 2x, bankStatement

Zoe began by recruiting a victim for her scam on the Moon with her typical solicitation, "do u want ur clamz doubled?" When the person responded positively, Zoe directed the person to Trade Room 49, then went there herself. A couple minutes later the person arrived and Zoe asked the Whyvillian to put all of his or her clams up for trade, "put up ur clamz plz," then said to press "agree" when she left her chair. Zoe then left her chair ("leave") and immediately went to check the result of the trade ("tradeResult"), checked her ymail and looked at someone's profile on City Records (perhaps her victim's?), then checked her bank statement. Because there was a trade result, we know the trade went through. That Zoe checked her bank statement afterward is another confirmation that she successfully obtained the poor Whyvillian's clams.

This rather intense scamming period lasted for only for a short time then disappeared from Zoe's Whyville life as quickly as it had started. We identified Zoe's scamming long after the fact when we looked at her logfiles. Even then, her multiple acts of scamming might have slipped our attention hadn't it been for a simple detail: the word "doubled" figured quite prominently in her chat comments. We didn't quite know what to make of that until we examined some of the chat interactions in more detail. We then also realized that Zoe was not the only player in the club who took on scamming. As we could tell from examining logfiles, other youth in the club also became involved in scamming, and then, like Zoe, moved on to other activities. In some ways, scamming could be seen as part of their efforts to become an insider on Whyville. It demonstrates their growing expertise; none of them started scamming right away when they began in Whyville. It took some time to learn the online lingo and practices, as illustrated in Zoe's exchanges at the Trading Post, to be recognized as an inside player. In the particular case of Zoe, she was a victim before becoming a perpetrator, imitating the practices of others. It is also one other way that her Whyville life was tied to her frequenting of the Trading Post and her interests in the financial opportunities in Whyville.

Others, like Blake, also engaged in boundary play, but in a different way. Blake turned out to be one of the more intense players on Whyville, though he didn't start out that way. In the first three months of his Whyville life, Blake primarily hung out with friends from the club in Whyville—both during and outside of club time. Like Brad and other boys, he organized projectile fights among club members on Whyville, flirted on occasion—and boasted of his flirtations in the club—and focused on designing his avatar. His conversation shifted seamlessly between chatting with friends like Brad in Whyville and in the club, and between conversations with school friends and flirting with or throwing projectiles at other Whyvillians.

After the club ended in early March, Blake's Whyville activities suddenly shifted. First he boosted his salary by focusing on salary-raising science games for a few weeks. Then he spent several days producing many face parts in the Face Factory, making eyes and other parts for sale. Finally, in mid-May, Blake's time[3] on Whyville suddenly quintupled, from around 60 to 90 minutes several days a week to 140 to 650 minutes every day for nearly a month. What explains this sudden intense shift in playing on Whyville? Two activities define this period, one old and one new. First, Blake continued to engage in a substantial amount of hanging out with friends he knew by name from school (mostly boys). Second, he began a new activity of trading in rare face parts. In Whyville, when one creates a face part, one chooses to "produce" a certain number of parts for a set price each, and sets a selling price for them. So if a face part sells out and the creator does not reproduce it, that part can only be obtained through trading. In this way, some parts on Whyville became rare and highly sought after, with Whyvillians paying large sums of clams for them. Blake tried to take advantage of this and spent a great deal of time seeking out parts by name ("ultimate," "time warp," "2% pink"), negotiating for them, and trying to sell them for even higher prices. Most of his efforts did not result in trades, but some did.

Blake's trading in rare face parts was a highly engaging activity that involved deep knowledge of fashion trends in Whyville, social negotiations with friends and many others he did not know, and financial machinations to get rich more quickly than his salary would allow. Indeed, in those final two months of the study, Blake started bragging about the amount of money he had. To friends, he often claimed that at one point he had 800k (800,000 clams) but that he was cheated and lost most of it; later he said that he had gotten back up to 640k. To others from whom he was trying to obtain rare face parts, he claimed to have 1.2 million or more clams, changing the numbers frequently and throwing out ridiculously large sums of money. Certainly some of his claims were exaggerations, but Whyvillians did exist who had millions in clams from face part sales. Blake had spent substantial time before his rare-trade hobby boosting his salary and making face parts to sell, so it is difficult to know how much money he actually had.

One striking thing about Blake is that connections with friends from school bled into his daily life in Whyville throughout his time there. Though he branched off in trading rare parts, his school ("real life") friends continued to play a role even in this. They asked him to make specific parts for them and discussed who was designing what so as not to flood the Whyville market with too many of their face parts. Thus, even when he was exploring the far ends of Whyville financial economies, he was still rooted in his everyday relationships with people he knew.

Not surprisingly, this is not something Zoe, Blake, or others discussed in their interviews at the end of the after-school club. Zoe did acknowledge in the interview that she had a few other Whyville accounts—a common way to earn more clams on Whyville (the second author even did this to earn enough for her first Whyville car), though she did not describe the way that she persistently begged people to give her accounts that already had high salaries—an activity she carried out about the same time that she began scamming people. Both of these activities, seeking multiple Whyville accounts and scamming others, are indications of Zoe's move toward being a Whyville insider, building up experiences with practices that were common on the site, including scamming. But her adoption of the questionable practice of scamming was also temporary, lasting only two weeks of the six-month duration of our study.

Good Play

In this chapter, we consider "boundary play" in the broad contexts of cheating and scamming, practices often condemned in society but viewed in a more nuanced way in gaming, where cheating may be common practice. Indeed, cheating and scamming are a regular part of life in Whyville. Go online and Google "cheats Whyville"—dozens if not hundreds of websites, and more recently video walkthroughs, appear in the search listings. The cheats and scams cover a wide range, from making guides for science games to identity theft for stealing people's passwords and accounts. Among players there is great variety on what counts as cheating, what the repercussions are, and how and when one should use cheats. There are regular ymail warnings against giving out one's password and newspaper articles alerting citizens to the latest clever innovations in scamming. The *Whyville Times* has numerous articles that debate the pros and cons of cheating and scamming. RJ's post about "ripping off Grandma" indicates that some believe that donated face parts should only serve for personal beautification, whereas others consider donated goods fair game for personal enrichment.

Cheating practices are so common in gaming that whole books have been written on the topic. Gaming researcher Mia Consalvo[4] argues that cheating allows players to build up "gaming capital" that provides them with key knowledge about how to be successful in the game. Indeed, most commercial games are surrounded by numerous cheat sites where players post explanations of how to complete various games, hints for how things work, and discovered or manufactured shortcuts through games. Even companies that would have the most interest in keeping cheats away from players often sponsor official guides that provide hints or outright answers for how to complete a game and forums where players post their own solutions or strategies. Some studies of these forums have documented scientific and mathematical thinking as players collaborate to strategize about gameplay.[5] A further complication is that the gaming industry's stance is much less lenient in regard to other player behaviors such as copying software or selling avatar parts. Thus, cheating is in fact part of the larger gaming culture in which players creatively push back on the designs and rules of the games imposed by the industry.

Cheating in school, on the other hand, has a very official different position: it is considered illegitimate but is widely practiced. Cheating is condemned because it presumes that the learner has solved a problem under false pretenses: another person or a borrowed source contributed to the solution rather than the learner's understanding. Recent studies of high school and college students report that the majority of them admit to practicing various forms of cheating such as copying texts and answers from exams.[6] This is one of the reasons why cheating offers a promising prospect to discuss ethics at large: the boundaries of what is legitimate are a moving target and are redefined by both individual players and community actions. These different perspectives of cheating create fertile grounds to challenge beliefs about what is legitimate and, more importantly, what it means to learn: in schools, individuals are seen as solely responsible for mastering the curricular content, whereas in games players' search for support from others is considered acceptable, if not crucial, for advancing in the game. Cheating, then, provides a vivid illustration of the different notions of learning assumed and valued in each community. In cheating, boundaries and norms are transgressed that not only concern ethical issues, but also touch at the core of learning.

No matter which side of cheating one considers, the boundary play that is the focus of this chapter connects with the larger issues of good play that have been the focus of a recent study by Harvard researchers.[7] In the report titled "Good Play," researchers examined the ethical "fault lines" that have emerged around digital media. The argument is that experiences in the digital world, positive or negative, provide pivotal learning moments. What it means to participate online in a meaningful and socially responsible way is "shaped by how they manage their identities and privacy, regard ownership and authorship, establish their credibility, treat others, and consider broader civic issues."[8] Zoe's scamming in order to get even or rich certainly crossed several of those fault lines, as victim and perpetrator. We don't know what Zoe took away from her scamming experiences, except that they took place during a crucial transitional period in her becoming a Whyville player. Others, like Blake, navigated these fault lines in more subtle ways, getting rich by amassing rare avatar parts.

Rather than judge Zoe's and Blake's actions, it might be more appropriate to situate their play in the larger ethical landscape of Whyville. In other words, we need to understand the particular norms and practices that emerged in this community to answer questions such as: How common is cheating and scamming in Whyville? What do other players in Whyville consider acceptable? What do they consider questionable? Is there consensus about good play in the community? To gain deeper insights into the ethos of Whyville, it is necessary to move beyond the boundaries of virtual worlds to the hundreds of cheat sites maintained by Whyville players on the Internet to construct and share cheats, that is, shortcuts to science games and tips on insider knowledge of virtual cultures. It is equally necessary to move back inside Whyville and examine public discussions of cheating and cheat sites illustrating the ways that good play crisscrosses the boundaries of digital life. But this is not all there is to cheating. Cheating in fact has a connection to learning that is rarely considered, a connection that moves beyond the ethical fault lines of right or wrong, and questions cheating from an educational perspective of what is being learned. In other words, we wonder whether games can be designed in such a fashion that developing cheats could become an opportunity rather than a shortcut for learning. We're fortunate to have captured one example in real time of how this can be possible. Later we report on how a collective of Whyville players worked on developing a cheat to a new science game over several months.

Cheating for All

The large number of cheat sites about Whyville is an indication of both Whyville's popularity and of the popularity of using cheats in Whyville. In July 2006 when we started looking at cheat sites, a few basic searches turned up 257 cheat sites, visible and available to anyone looking. A cursory search today reveals as many if not more sites, including new ones updated regularly as new games in Whyville are released. As a first attempt at understanding the range of cheats available for Whyville, we applied Katie Salen and Erik Zimmerman's typology of cheats in games[9] to uncover the types of cheats in Whyville. We have outlined their definitions in table 5.1 and listed parallel types of cheats found on Whyville sites.

To illustrate, an Easter egg is something hidden into the design of the game itself, such as a secret room in the game space. Whyville has its own set of unlisted spaces in the game meant to be uncovered, including Earth, Jupiter, Moon, Saturn, and Mars. Similar to Easter eggs, designers also develop cheat codes with the intention that they will be discovered (or read about in a gaming magazine) and shared with others. These codes might allow a player to have unlimited magic power or special jumping abilities.

Table 5.1
Typology of Whyville cheats.

Cheats	Description	Whyville Cheats
Easter eggs	Special secrets hidden in the game by designers	Unlisted spaces within the game, e.g., Jupiter, Disco Room, the Newspaper
Cheat codes	Actual codes written up the designers (providing immortality and other benefits)	Indirect parallels in Whyville: "teleport Jupiter" to get to Jupiter, "earmuffs now on" to listen to people whispering online
Game guides and walkthroughs	Step-by-step instruction for finishing a game	Most common on cheat sites: How to play through a game Answers to games Illustrations for games
Workarounds	"Legal" ways of working around game structures	E.g., House of Illusions: walking through all rooms without looking at anything Setting up another account to get more clams Selling or buying others' extra accounts
True cheating	Really and truly breaking the official site rules (e.g. multisessioning)	Stealing others' accounts through scams that ask for usernames and passwords
Hacks	Intervention on the level of a computer code	Codes that deposit many clams in an account (now expired—we were unable to test these)
Spoilsport hacking	Intervening in a way that brings down the game and does not promote the purpose of being involved in the games	Stealing others' accounts by hacking into the system (there were rumors of this happening but it was unstudied by the authors)

In Whyville, we find a parallel in a few simple computer commands typed into one's chat bubble such as "teleport moon," a code that transports one to the Moon on Whyville (described in chapter 2), or "earmuffs now on," a code that allows players to eavesdrop on private whispered conversations. "Walkthroughs" and "walkarounds" are strategies developed or discovered by players to accomplish difficult tasks in a game.

In Whyville, a walkthrough might consist of step-by-step instructions on how to play through a level of a science game, while a walkaround consists of a trick that allows one to get around some work intended by the game designers. For instance, in Whyville's House of Illusions, players are supposed to walk through a set of rooms and spend time looking at optical illusions in each room. Finishing each room results in an increase to one's salary in increments of one. However, it is possible, using a cheat, to walk through all the rooms without actually bothering to look at anything and still get a whopping eight-clam salary raise. Similarly, one might create a second account on Whyville to earn money and send it to one's main account. This allows the player to accumulate virtual wealth more quickly.

Salen and Zimmerman differentiate between the types of cheating described above and what they call "true cheating," hacks, and spoilsport cheating. These forms of cheating go beyond finding secret places and accidents in the design of the game. Players who engage in these practices usually are not interested in the goals of the game (finishing a game or, in Whyville, earning a good salary in order to hang out with others) but in negatively affecting the experiences of others. For instance, it is a frequent practice in Whyville to lie to Whyvillians in order to obtain their password so that one can log into their account and send the money to oneself. This type of cheating, and other hacks or computer codes developed by users to intervene in the game programming itself, affects the gaming environment negatively for others, at least in multiplayer games.

Cheats in Whyville are discovered by kids for kids. So as a further look into this practice we looked at the different kinds of cheat sites kids were making.[10] At first glance, the cheat sites varied in the number of games for which they posted cheats, but we found that the quality of cheats—the directions, explanations, and illustrations they provided for solving a game—were much more important in categorizing the sites. Indeed, only a few of the cheat sites we studied provided almost complete listings for games, including solutions for the hard levels of certain games, and researched some answers outside of Whyville. These sites also supplied insider tips for participating on the site, including which shops offered the best face parts, how to teleport to secret locations not listed on the normal Whyville map, and even a computer code to throw projectiles more quickly and thus get the best of your opponents. They also included contributions from multiple players, in contrast to other websites that were compiled solely by individuals.

In comparison, several more sites provided solutions for four to ten games and included in their solutions some directions or illustrations that facilitated completing games. At the lower end were sites with cheats that only gave unexplained or incomplete answers to games, such as a list of answers without explanations of how to implement them. While lists of answers worked for some games, this did not help with other games. For instance, the Great Balloon Race requires players to fly between altitude levels with different wind directions in order to drop a sandbag on a target and then safely land. Poor cheats for this game only provided the altitudes in which one needed to fly in each level, information that is not very helpful in actually flying the hot air balloon. Better cheats offered more explicit directions, such as how to navigate between altitude levels where the wind switches directions, and even provided screenshots of the levels.

Finally, a number of cheat sites were exact copies of other cheat sites, identifiable by use of identical language and punctuation in their solutions. These appeared to be cut-and-pasted, plagiarized websites.[11] Other sites were scams, soliciting individuals' passwords with promises to increase their salary or put money in their accounts. These sites, especially the scam sites, violate models of good play, and constitute what Salen and Zimmerman would call "true cheating," rather than sharing strategies for how to play.

One commonality among less comprehensive cheat sites (but not the scams) was that they were also personal webpages. In other words, these were the personal websites of kids who played on Whyville and wanted to display their knowledge about Whyville as part of their personal website. Many of these websites were either unfinished or were part of a larger personal website. This may provide clues as to the motivations of the website designers in featuring the cheats—displaying knowledge and affiliation about Whyville as part of their personal identifies on their websites. It is also encouraging to see that many young people made an effort to create a website, even if they did not finish it.

Interestingly enough, during our investigation we found a website where a Whyvillian compiled an independent evaluation of cheat sites. As part of his own cheat site, this player had assembled a page listing thirty-eight other cheat sites and rated them with one to five stars, sometimes with comments about which sites were scams. In general our typology agreed with his; we agreed on which sites were scams, and his star rating system correlated with our own rankings. We thoroughly agreed on his only four- and five-star ratings, which matched with the two sites we evaluated as the best. His only five-star-rated cheat site also happened to be the site we chose for continued study, GameSite.net.[12] During the time we followed activities on this website, the appearance of the Spitzer Spectrometer, a new salary-raising game on Whyville, provided a rare opportunity to witness and study the collective and public development of a new cheat (see chapter 7).

Community Views on Cheating

If Zoe and other players scammed under a veil of secrecy, Whyvillians openly discuss this central part of digital life in the *Whyville Times*, the weekly online serial that constitutes a community forum where players debate the ethics of cheating games, cheating players, cheating in elections, and cheating on virtual boyfriends. As in the commercial gaming world,[13] cheating is a hotly debated topic in Whyville, and the newspaper articles criticize the practice of using cheat sites to increase salaries illegitimately: "When just one person uses cheats it could affect our whole town," writes one author.[14] Yet the conversation goes beyond simple condemnation of using cheats, though many of the writers espouse that view.

Our search of the archive identified over 100 articles that mentioned cheats in the *Whyville Times* from 2000 to 2005. Roughly ten of them were explicit warnings against scams, reporting on the many imaginative ways Whyvillians have tried to procure others' passwords with the promise of raising their salaries, giving them makeovers, and even claiming to be site designers. About one-third of the articles more generally condemned cheating in salary-raising games, such as using cheats found on cheat sites like GameSite.net. Others discussed cheating in the Smart Cars races where instead of going around the track as in a traditional race, some players would immediately turn their cars around and cross the finish line, thus triggering a win. These particular articles constituted a long, multiyear discussion about whether this was a valid way to win at Smart Cars. Some utterly denounced the practice, while others, including the *Times* editor, considered it a rather clever method. Still another ten of the articles concerned cheating in dating relationships, some of them asking whether it was cheating if one had one boyfriend in the "real" world and a different one in Whyville. Another twenty concerned issues with ballot stuffing, creating multiple accounts in order to have more votes for oneself in elections for Whyville senator or prom king/queen. And a final ten described and rebuked other forms of cheating in Whyville, including the provocative "ripping off Grandma" showcased in the introductory vignette in this chapter.

By far the predominant view of cheating in the articles is that cheating is bad, lazy, dishonest, and unfair. In addition, they claim that it hurts Whyville and goes against the "Whyville Way," a philosophy that values learning, mutual support, and contributing in positive ways to the community. Many of the arguments are based on the idea that such practices are wrong in real life and therefore are also wrong in virtual life: "On Whyville you have to earn your things and earn a living, just like in real life" (Twigsy 2002). This and many other articles espoused the view that morals in "real" life should apply to virtual life, arguing that people should directly connect values in one place to those in another.

In addition to "stealing from Grandma," we discovered seemingly innumerable other types of cheating in Whyville that we could not have imagined on our own. Some of the more interesting cheats included obtaining passwords by offering "makeovers," copying face parts (a designer/copyright issue), and creatively coordinating cussing. For this latter cheat, GrriesYEA[15] vividly described three citizens standing next to each other, saying:

Person 1:   Bu
Person 2:   tt
Person 3:   head

He goes on to denounce this and other forms of cussing, consisting of creative spellings of bad words, that try to get around the censorship word filter on Whyville.

But not all Whyvillians consider cheating as completely negative. Though not in the majority, many writers saw intellectual and creative elements in cheating practices on Whyville (see our previous discussions about cheating in the Smart Cars game). Regarding more traditional salary-raising cheats, some writers pointed out how those cheats could be useful in getting people to the next step of their participation in Whyville:

> And how many of you got help earning your salary, whether from a friend or by using a cheat site? (Kemario 2005)

> Some of us are unable to complete the games, and it is tough finding help (there is a cheat site but its name will not be released). (LukeG 2002)

Indeed, we witnessed a site designer publicly confessing to having used a cheat during a community discussion at the Greek Theater, the live public forum in Whyville. So even the game designers use cheats once in a while![16]

The large number of articles devoted to discussing cheating, roughly one every three weeks, demonstrates that players are aware of cheating in Whyville. What are some of the effects of cheating on this virtual community? Beyond just the existence of the debate of cheats in Whyville, one of the most evident effects is disillusionment about elections and leaders in Whyville. The issue of ballot stuffing and bribing voters comes up almost every Senate election, to the point that some Whyvillians formed a committee to try to dissolve elections. Several authors in the *Times* have discussed the challenge of how many votes should be allowed to those with multiple Whyville accounts. In such cases, should votes be counted by accounts or by the person behind the count? Some argued that multiple accounts used by the same individual should be allowed one vote each if the accounts represent active citizens in Whyville. Yet at times new accounts have been created in order to cheat elections. In fact, one Senate campaigner purposely cheated in an election just to bring the issue to the forefront:

> I wanted to prove that everyone who gets lots of votes is a cheater. And that even though the accounts behind it might not be obvious, a majority of the accounts are from the same select few people.[17]

Her "secret experiment" certainly worked to publicize the view that ballot stuffing is a frequent enterprise on Whyville (though notably she was "caught," so perhaps it is not as easy to do as she thought). In addition, with the availability of cheats to raise one's salary, one of the qualifications for being a citizen-leader in Whyville, namely being a "ymail helper," is called into question. Several writers doubted whether ymail helpers were truly qualified to help newbies, since they may not have actually played the games to earn a salary. While these issues may or may not be as prevalent as some citizens think, the cynicism in the public forum of Whyville is apparent in the vast majority of the articles we read.

Learning to Cheat—Cheating to Learn

In this last section, we want to turn our attention to another aspect of cheating, one that is less concerned with ethical implications and more interested in the learning opportunities associated with cheating. While this is an uncommon view, we believe it is one that potentially has great benefits for those interested in bringing gaming into education. Our examinations of some of the cheat sites and the cheat development at GameSite .net revealed a great deal about designers' learning processes. Except for the scammers, all of the cheat site designers were invested in Whyville, in promoting others' success on Whyville, and in displaying their knowledge of Whyville. They viewed the object of the "game" as getting a salary to buy face parts and participate in the larger Whyvillian culture. They valued the morals of Whyville, displayed in qualifiers to their chat cheats, asking viewers to read carefully and understand the principles behind the chat license questions. Still further, they took the time to learn the inside secrets of Whyville. In addition, the designers often did substantial research to develop their sites and to learn how to complete the science games. This includes technological research (Web development, HTML, short codes) and scientific research (illustrations of spectra, theories about spinning fast).

What if we analyzed Whyville games in light of the cheats that can be developed for them? Would that help us to design educational games that could provide rich affordances for deeper science inquiry? Consider the Alien Rescue game, a rich game about spatial relations between the Sun and the Earth and the causes of the seasons, where requiring just simple answers would remove all richness from the game; or the House of Illusions game, where players simply walk around and look at different illusions to complete it. The most common type of cheat is a list of answers or screenshots (pictures) that show a "correct" way to finish a game level. The basic skill for using this kind of cheat is similar to having a list of answers for a multiple-choice test; one only has to type in or choose the correct answer from a list provided to finish the game. This generally leaves very little potential for learning. For instance, the Alien Rescue game involves complex three-dimensional thinking about the Earth rotating on its axis and revolving around the Sun in addition to hints about the people in a certain part of the world in order to identify a place at a certain time of year. But when a game can be solved with a list of answers, what can be learned from the cheats? How might we design games for *educational* cheats?

Consider instead the Zero Gravity game, which is similar to the 1970s children's toy Simon, where one must remember and punch four lights in a particular order based on the order in which they originally blinked. The only difference is that in the Zero Gravity game one must throw objects in order to propel oneself to hit each light (see figure 5.1).

Throwing objects at a certain angle, from zero to 359 degrees, results in moving a short distance in the opposite direction according to Newton's third law of equal and opposite reaction. In other words, throwing a smiley projectile to zero degrees, or to the right in Whyville, causes one to move directly left; in the game zero is right, 90 is down, 180 is left, and 270 is up. The cheats for this game gave explicit directions about how to

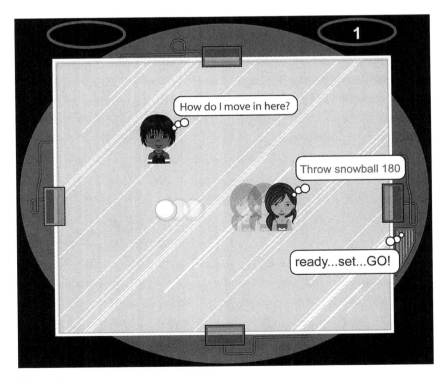

Figure 5.1
The Zero Gravity game.

use projectiles to make oneself move in the opposite direction of a throw (rephrasing Whyville's more formal directions in the players' own words), suggested that one buy 200 to 300 projectiles in order to complete all ten levels (something one author wished she had known when she first played the game), and even included a picture of every five-degree angle in a circle (see figure 5.2 for a similar image). The picture of angles was a very helpful reference that might aid players in their speed of recalling which angle would cause them to move in which direction.

In an interesting turn, these cheats can reveal how much there is to experiment with and explore within a game. Certain games do not lend themselves to a list of answers. Instead, the cheats for such games consist of walkthroughs, perhaps with helpful reference guides or pictures on the more comprehensive cheat sites. Notably, relatively few cheat sites we studied gave walkthroughs or guides for the more difficult games. In fact, only GameSite.net provided cheats for all of the salary-raising science games in Whyville, including a number of cheats not available on other sites. More importantly, these observations suggest that educational games could be designed in such a way that they might require more research and not simple answers, encouraging players to draw in research from other sites (texts, websites, experts) and contribute to the knowledge of the larger community.

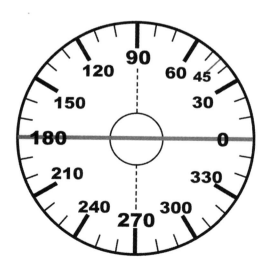

Figure 5.2
Zero Gravity cheat reference.

Here, then, is upside-down way thinking: why not design games to promote "good" cheating? Cheating can support collaborative problem-solving skills, help players to think about the design of games, and sponsor research and technical skills. Games that require only simple cheats do not provide rich opportunities for learning, whereas those that involve complex cheats move beyond just memorizing facts to requiring cheaters and players alike to engage in deeper, often collaborative inquiry. Let's apply this to learning environments in general. What if we designed learning environments to sponsor cheating? One of the authors challenged her graduate students to "cheat" in her course one semester, providing in-class time for students to share cheats and shortcuts. What students came up with was a list of strategies for reading articles, planning final papers, managing time, and sharing their interpretations about different topics in the course.

We are not alone in thinking that such approaches to cheating can indeed lead to better learning opportunities. Yrjo Engeström[18] used a similar approach in one of his courses, encouraging students to use cheat cards on tests and collecting the cards at the end to analyze them for learning strategies. Likewise, Donald Norman[19] argued in the "defense of cheating" that we should "change the educational system to make it more relevant to the world, to teach proper skills, and at the same time eliminate the deceitful, hidden acts of cheating by recognizing cheating for the good that it brings: group activities towards a common goal." Turning boundary play into good play provides a fruitful context to consider how to engage kids in learning to play thoughtfully, creatively, and responsibly.

6 Science Play

Run for the hills, bounce to the CDC,
It doesn't matter what you do,
this virus ALWAYS gets the best of you.
Whether you're sat on, whispered to or get a kiss,
You never win against this blotchy abyss.
They say they got rid of rashes, and annoying pimply things!
But they're all over everyone's face, the size of diamond rings!
"Achoo" say all the avatars in the contaminated room,
the pox is spreading to EVERYONE like a giant cloud of doom.
And now the myths commence of how to end this horror.
You can buy all the cover-ups and contribute all you want, but you'll find you're
only getting poorer.
Some people cheer the pox on. Others protest and say: "Booooo!"
But either way they got sadder, as the pimples grew and grew.
WhyPox has engulfed this fair town like a giant wormhole in space.
But just as everyone thinks it's the end of Whyville, it disapears without a trace.
When the pimples go away, we all think that it's the end.
But wait 12 months, and there you go, the pox has returned. AGAIN.
—Theboy2, Whyville Poet[1]

"Why, Why, Why Pox?"

WhyPox, the outbreak described above by self-proclaimed Whyville poet Theboy2, is a virtual epidemic that appears annually in Whyville, corresponding to the time of the actual flu season. During the outbreaks of WhyPox, infected Whyvillians show two symptoms: red pimples appeared on their avatars and sneezing interrupted their chat, with "sneezing" and the word "achoo" appearing amid their chat phrases. Numedeon intended the WhyPox epidemic for educational purposes. Players could track their disease in community graphs in a virtual CDC (a Center for Disease Control) in Whyville, post theories about its cause and transmission mechanisms, and make predictions about when the epidemic would end. They could also run simulations of the epidemic and discuss the epidemic in articles in the *Whyville Times*, like the one written by Theboy2. While most epidemic outbreaks don't inspire poems, his writings do capture many facets of the phenomenon—the possible disease vectors and various attempts to hide or cheer on the WhyPox outbreak.

In early 2005, we initiated and observed an outbreak of WhyPox to understand better participants' learning experiences inside and outside of school. Aidan (screen name: masher47), one of Zoe's club mates, was one of the first club players who experienced the WhyPox outbreak. On February 5, a Saturday afternoon, Aidan logged on and stayed in Whyville for a full ninety minutes. Almost immediately after logging in, he teleported to Mars and saw a friend from the club, Trevor. Then he engaged in his typical practice of making friends and flirting with potential girlfriends by going around Whyville and saying "hi" or "asl" (age-sex-location).

After a couple of minutes, he noticed someone sneeze ("Achoo!") and whispered "bless you." Quickly noticing that many people were sneezing, he traveled rapidly around Whyville, going to the Moon and then back to Mars to see if the sneezing was happening everywhere and asking broadly in chat, "what is wrong with everyone?"

Ten minutes after he first went online, he realized that he himself had caught WhyPox, as "Achoo" started appearing in his chat and whispers. It even interrupted his teleporting; when he typed "teleport moon," it appeared as "Achooteleport moon," and he had to retype the command in his chat bubble in order to get to the Moon. He even noticed another Whyvillian who started to say "Achoo" immediately after talking with him and asked, "Achoo did i get you sick."

Thus, within fifteen minutes of going online, masher47 noticed that people were sneezing, and though he at first thought they were doing it on purpose, quickly realized that something strange was going on in Whyville. He explored the phenomenon, traveling about Whyville and asking others what was happening. He quickly caught the virus himself and began to wonder out loud whether he had caused someone else to get sick. WhyPox successfully caught masher47's attention within minutes, elicited his curiosity, and even promoted some thinking about causality and transmission of the virus.

In this chapter, we will examine more closely the opportunities for learning science in virtual worlds, starting with the virtual WhyPox epidemic and then moving on to other examples of community science games that focus on nutrition and ecology. We argue that community science games realize some of the research and educational potential that William Bainbridge[2] foresaw in virtual environments, leveraging real-time participation of a massive number of players that can reach into the millions. In the case of a virtual epidemic outbreak, we can infect and study whole player populations without the players actually experiencing any physical harm. Only players' avatars and actions are affected, which of course can create a great deal of frustration or excitement, but it also serves as a powerful motivator to learn about infectious diseases and understand viable pathways to mitigate their spread among large-scale communities. Unlike reading in a textbook about historical plagues, participation in a virtual epidemic gives students a first-hand and real-time experience of key aspects of infectious diseases. What does it feel and look like to live and learn in the times of a virtual epidemic outbreak? Before we can address this question, let's talk about designing WhyPox, which after all is a human-made event.

Designing a Virtual Epidemic

Planning an epidemic is a challenging task. How will the disease spread? What should the symptoms be? How long will they last? One of the first things to do when designing a virtual epidemic is to determine the disease vectors—how the infection will spread in the community. As in real life, viruses can spread in different ways, from airborne to touch or ingestion, modes of transmission that are challenging but not impossible to implement online. Frequency of transmission is also important; how often do individuals have to come into contact with a virus to become infected? Further, one's chances of becoming infected also ought to depend on general health. Though people often believe that any encounter with a sick person will make them infected, this is not always the case.[3] Infection also depends on how virulent the virus is and whether the infected person will stay alive long enough to infect others. Diseases like Ebola have such a high mortality rate that most infected individuals die before they can transmit the disease. All of these aspects, from transition to virulence as well as people's general health actions, preventive or not, translate into probabilities that all factor into how an epidemic runs its course.

In order to plan for an epidemic that would be both educational and engaging, we first ran a number of silent simulations of WhyPox.[4] In silent simulations, players don't actually see or experience the outbreak while they go about their daily life. From behind the scenes, designers observe how quickly the virus spreads, though without any intentional human activities involved. This spread is captured in the community graph (see figure 6.1).

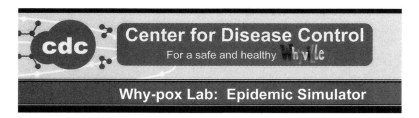

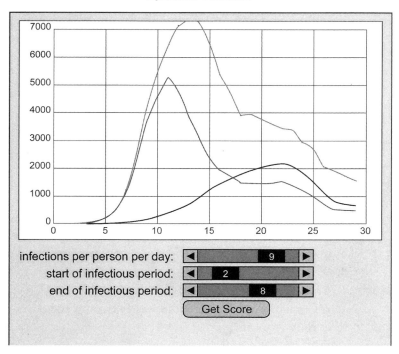

Figure 6.1
WhyPox community graph.

For educational purposes, we wanted to design an outbreak that would capture Whyvillians' curiosity and provide them with ample time to speculate about possible causes of the disease, share their knowledge with others, and possibly take action against infection. For this reason, after several attempts at modeling the virus, we created a WhyPox that would spread over a matter of weeks (rather than spiking within a few hours and then dying out). We set a low probability of getting infected and chose two transmission mechanisms: proximity to someone already infected and length of time spent in that proximal space. We kept the sneezing and red pimples as visible signs of infection because they mimicked popular diseases such as the common cold and chickenpox. Then we set up a discussion forum, a virtual Center for Disease Control (CDC) with graphs of infection rates, and elicited articles for the weekly online serial the *Whyville Times* for Whyvillians to glean and share knowledge. These combined factors led to a successful virtual epidemic, one that affected a large portion of the Whyville population not simply with a virus, but with a need-to-know curiosity about what was happening.

Living in the Times of WhyPox

As WhyPox hit Whyville, it had an immediate effect on Whyvillians, largely because it manifested in the two most popular activities: designing avatars and chatting. The first symptom of WhyPox is the outbreak of pimples on avatars' faces, which intensify and then recede over time as the disease fades away (see figure 6.2). As one after-school club member, Bryce, complained, the pimples spread all over the faces, necks, and even hair of kids' avatars, "Dot dot dot on the neck, dot dot dot on the body." This irritated many Whyvillians who prided themselves on creating good-looking avatars. The second symptom is the random punctuation of chat with an "Achoo," interrupting conversation and even hampering some actions done through chat in Whyville, like teleporting and throwing projectiles. Where normally someone could type "throw mudball masher47," whereby a mudball would travel from the thrower to the intended target before the target saw the throw-command, with WhyPox it might come out as "Achoothrow mudball masher47," which meant that the mudball would not travel and the intended target would have warning of the attack.

Figure 6.2
WhyPox outbreak at Leila's patio (above) and the CDC.

Although these features of WhyPox infection may at first seem funny or merely a nuisance, they interrupted valued social functions and activities and for that reason caught the immediate attention of many players.

The WhyPox virus spread fairly quickly and within three days of its launch the disease had peaked and infected more than 4,000 community members. Technically, there wasn't an exact end point for the virtual epidemic; the absence of spots and achoos eventually indicated that the outbreak had been eradicated. During the outbreak, Whyvillians freely offered advice and folk cures for WhyPox just as they shared other insider expertise. It was at this point that the virtual CDC established in Whyville became an informational hub for the community (see figure 6.3). Visits to the virtual CDC before the outbreak of WhyPox were close to nonexistent, with the exception of the occasional curious peek or accidental visit by players. This all changed once WhyPox arrived, with the number of visits jumping to 5,386 within two weeks as Whyvillians sought, shared, and analyzed information about the virus that had spread among them.

The Whyville virtual CDC contains several features:

• An opening screen with a live-updated graph visualizing levels of infection throughout the community.

• An archive with information about previous infections.

• An Infection Simulator where Whyvillians can adjust a variable of how many infections one person can make per day, to estimate the rate of spread of the disease.

• A more complex Epidemic Simulator where players adjust three variables: infections per person per day, start of infectious period, and end of infectious period (i.e., how long an infection would last). The Epidemic Simulator requires Whyvillians to make predictions based on their variable choices for how long the disease will last in Whyville and how quickly it will spread.

• Outbreak Headquarters where Whyvillians can read three cases of Whyvillians becoming infected and suggest explanations for the vectors of disease spread. Players can also submit their own medical case histories of WhyPox and by looking at many cases make suggestions about how the disease is spreading.

• A bulletin board where players post predictions about the causes of WhyPox and when it will go away.

Why-pox Lab: Epidemic Simulator

Epidemic Simulator

Please predict what will happen in the simulation:

How many days will the epidemic last?

◄ 21 ►

What day will the epidemic peak?

◄ 15 ►

What percentage of people will be infected on the peak day?

◄ 50% ►

What percentage of the people will have been infected at the end of the simulation?

◄ 80% ►

Why do you think this is what will happen?

I made my guesses based on the WhyPox epidemic we had last year.

Submit

Figure 6.3
Whyville Center for Disease Control.

In postings at the CDC, most Whyvillians agreed that people got better within two weeks, but there was greater variety in their predictions about how WhyPox was spread. Common responses suggested WhyPox spread from chatting or ymailing someone who was infected, by getting hit with a projectile from an infected person, or just being in the same place as other infected people. Others thought one became infected from the Sun or not wearing warm virtual clothes when it was cold outside. In fact, scarves became popular items in Whyville because the rumor spread that they could keep players from getting sick. The variety of responses elicited many arguments and counterarguments, with debaters often citing as evidence experiences of those who engaged in activities that allegedly should have infected them but didn't. From this point of view, the bulletin boards and forum discussions were successful in facilitating Whyvillians' observations and theorizing about the transmission of WhyPox.

At the same time that WhyPox was peaking, articles begin to appear in the *Whyville Times* about the epidemic. In the February 6 and February 13, 2005 issues, when WhyPox was the most prevalent, three of twenty and five of twenty-one articles, respectively, concerned WhyPox. In these articles, authors discussed when and where they discovered WhyPox, theories for how it was transmitted, and even a scam where some Whyvillians offered to "heal" those infected if only they would be given passwords to accounts so that they could use their "computer genius" to cure people. Some even wrote poems about it, like the one by Theboy2 quoted at the beginning of this chapter. Interestingly, many authors reported discovering WhyPox the same way that masher47 did. They saw it in one place and thought it might be a joke, then went to another place and realized that something different was happening. As one writer described it: "Other times before this morning, people would go around faking the WhyPox and saying Achoo. I played along this morning, fake sneezing like everyone else. But little did I know, they were sneezing beyond their control."[5]

By all accounts, WhyPox influenced much of Whyville life, from movements to social interactions to preventive behaviors, even virtual clothes shopping. In this sense, WhyPox was a major community event in Whyville, shaping players' everyday activities. Contagion was a concern for many players who said that WhyPox's infectious nature made it very realistic. Many of the surveyed players said that if WhyPox came back, Whyvillians should isolate themselves to prevent the spread. The practice of isolating oneself and avoiding others who had the virus was a common practice during the outbreak. As Brad, an after-school club member, summed up, "Some people with WhyPox would go to the mall so I would go to another place so I wouldn't catch it." Although some didn't change their interactions with others, social ostracism did occur. Another after-school club member, Scott, described how he felt when people avoided him when he was infected:

I mean it wasn't that great cause, uh, no one really trades or gets near you, and what's that word … You can't chat with people because if you had WhyPox and another person had WhyPox you can both chat with each other but if you … if this other person doesn't have WhyPox he's not going to want to talk to you cause he doesn't want to get the WhyPox.

WhyPox also evoked sentiments of compassion. As one online player related, "It made me feel like if someone made fun of another dude/ett everyone would have ypox and everyone would stick together. And help that one person cause it doesnt just affect that person it affects everyone with WhyPox around that same person. And I felt I was proud of having ypox at that time." This is reminiscent of Lofgren and Fefferman's observations of players in World of Warcraft that revealed empathy through shared experience of a viral outbreak.[6]

Infecting thousands of players' avatars with a disease that resembles acne and makes socialization more awkward raises ethical concerns, especially given the developmental priorities of our mostly tween players. We do know from the surveys that most players disliked it: over 60 percent said WhyPox made them feel bad and close to 40 percent said it hurt their social interactions, while almost a quarter saw nothing positive about it at all. One could argue that educational game designers should not be allowed to inflict this kind of misery onto young players just for the sake of science learning. Although players' avatars did not die, as they did in the case of the World of Warcraft outbreak, we do need to acknowledge that numerous players felt that their interactions on Whyville were negatively affected. We do think, however, that debriefings such as writing in the *Whyville Times* about the experience can help mitigate some of these negative experiences. We also note that in its current variant, WhyPox is a permanent feature of Whyville life and players have the opportunity to design a vaccine for protection—features not available at the time we conducted the study.

Clearly, WhyPox generated many different kinds of feelings and actions on the part of players. But what did Whyvillians learn, if anything, from this experience? How can we connect this to the science learning—asking questions, making observations, developing theories, and testing hypotheses—that is valued by science educators?

Learning about the "Why" in "WhyPox"

One of the advantages of a popular, open, and educational virtual world is that kids and educators can use it in many ways to promote learning. We studied several ways that Whyville connected kids to science—on its own with its embedded science tools to understand WhyPox, in the after-school club where kids could talk to each other both in Whyville and in person, and in a classroom where we designed a curriculum to accompany the WhyPox epidemic. Here, we first describe the simulator tools designed for Whyvillians to develop scientific understandings of the WhyPox epidemic in Whyville, and follow this with some examples from our studies of kids' learning science through WhyPox in each of the scenarios listed above—from Whyville, to the club, and finally to the classroom.

Investigating Science/Investigating WhyPox

As mentioned earlier, several science simulators were put into place in Whyville at the virtual CDC to accompany the WhyPox outbreak. In particular, the simulators were intended to help kids make the jump from thinking about the WhyPox epidemic specifically to how epidemics run their course more generically. We tracked the numbers of uses of the simulators and found that the frequency of simulator use peaked during the outbreak: over 1,400 simulations were performed. Further, while many players simply tried out the simulator just once, more than one-sixth (116/595) of our consenting online players engaged in more systematic investigations by running the simulations three or more times.[7] This rate of more systematic investigations is highly encouraging. Since the consenting participants represented the breadth of the Whyville population, it is a good sign that thousands of kids were likely to run the simulator multiple times. But what might kids learn by playing through the simulator more than once?

By examining the predictions that Whyvillians made from one round of simulation use to the next, we can get a sense of the extent to which they improved their understanding of the principles of how infectious disease spreads. Half of those players who completed three or more rounds of the simulation demonstrated significant improvements in the accuracy of their predictions. There are two ways to understand this improvement.[8] Players can adopt a scientific approach and try to improve their understanding of the *general* principles involved, making their predictions more accurate for any set of conditions within the simulation. They can also adopt an engineering approach by trying to create a certain outcome of the epidemic. They do this by keeping conditions fairly constant from round to round except for simple adjustments of their predictions according to the result that they are trying to create, like infecting the most or the least numbers of people in a certain period of time. By comparing the patterns of players' adjustments of the variables in the simulators to the accuracy of their predictions, we can draw inferences about the type of investigative goal each player pursued.

We found that the actions of 70 percent of the Whyville players reflected an engineering approach in using the simulators rather than a more general scientific approach. This suggests that most players who engaged with the simulations were not pursuing an abstract scientific understanding of the phenomena but instead were trying to achieve specific results within the simulations. This engineering orientation is reminiscent of applied research studies intended to address specific problems, such as identifying strategies for reducing the likelihood of infection. It also resembles investigative play, with Whyvillians trying to "push the limits" of the simulation to see how they could get the most people infected in a short period of time or how they could minimize the effects of the epidemic. Both of these interpretations point to a socially grounded motivation for use of the simulations in the virtual CDC in contrast to a more conventional, academic goal of theory-testing. Whyvillians who learned through repeated use of the simulators (about $1/12$ of those in our sample) did so in highly social ways. Building on this socially motivated learning, we now turn to casual conversations for evidence of informal science learning in Whyville, the club, and the class.

Talking Science—Talking WhyPox in the Club

In 1990, science educator Jay Lemke published the seminal book *Talking Science* in which he examined classroom discussions between science teachers and students. Lemke particularly focused on how scientific argumentation—a cornerstone of what it means to think and act like a scientist—was embedded in those interchanges. In Lemke's words, "Learning science means learning to *talk* science," and talking science means "observing, classifying, analyzing, discussing, hypothesizing, theorizing, questioning, challenging, arguing ... with the language of science."[9] One way that we sought to evaluate what Whyvillians had learned was simply to see if their language changed during the WhyPox epidemic—did they use different words when the epidemic hit? Indeed, after studying Whyvillians' chat before, during, and after the outbreak of WhyPox, we found that the words "pox," "sick," and "spot" suddenly spiked during the epidemic and slowly petered out after everyone had recovered.[10] So, WhyPox changed the words kids used in Whyville; what other kinds of conversations did it stimulate?

To answer this question, we decided to look more closely at informal conversations in the after-school club to see if kids' language had changed in more significant ways, particularly if they were *arguing* about the WhyPox epidemic.[11] Since the club was loosely organized—it was simply a free-play situation where kids played on Whyville—we thought it would be a good place to see if kids' everyday language had become scientific in any way. As a matter of fact, it had. During the epidemic, kids started arguing in scientific ways: debating who was infected, discussing the spread of the virus, and theorizing about prevention using their own experiences as well as their observations of the Whyville community at large.[12] This is an exciting form of scientific inquiry. Kids experiencing the epidemic did not have authoritative sources to draw on for answers like a doctor or a parent. Instead, they debated among themselves, putting together clues about the virus, contagion, and infection.

Arguing about whether someone was infected was a particularly frequent topic of conversation. The following is an example of how one group of three youth in the after-school club reacted to and argued about the status of a boy's possible infection with WhyPox:

Blake: Hey Dude, don't get me sick.
Scott: You're already sick man.
Blake: No, I'm not.
Scott: Yes you are, look, where are you.
Blake: I'm right here.
Scott: That's you?
Blake: Yeah I changed me [i.e., his avatar].
Leslie: Where are you?
Blake: Right here.
Leslie: Oh, you're not saying ahchoo.
Blake: I know, I don't have the WhyPox ...

In this conversation, Blake, Scott, and Leslie argued about whether Blake was infected with WhyPox. They observed his avatar (whose outfit he had changed recently) and noticed that he wasn't saying "Achoo" (he also didn't show any red pimples). After this observation and momentary debate about the evidence (or lack thereof), they decided that since he did not exhibit the symptoms of WhyPox, he didn't have it.

Besides arguing about infection status, youth also discussed strategies for dealing with symptoms and the duration of symptoms. Quite a range of opinions concerning the infection's cause emerged, including whispering with an infected Whyvillian, sending ymail, throwing projectiles, or even buying infected face parts, as well as many others. The leading claim suggested that being too close to an infected Whyvillian would cause infection, akin to getting the "Cooties" from sitting too close to an undesirable classmate. Below is an example of this from an exchange between youth when uninfected club members on Whyville saw avatars with WhyPox moving close to theirs:

Paul: Ahh too many sick people. Get away. Aidan, you're achooing. There's a girl with WhyPox following me! Ahh … !
Scott: There's a lot of people saying Achoo.
Aidan: Woo hoo I gave you WhyPox!
Paul: What?! Nuh uh.
Aidan: Yeah huh.
Paul: You don't see freckles on me.
Aidan: Yeah but guess what, tomorrow you are.

This casual banter between club members became a more substantial argument when we consider the implicit elements of their conversation. Both Paul and Aidan shared the generally accepted notion that proximity increases the probability of getting infected. They also shared the understanding that pimples (referred to as "freckles" in this case) are a symptom of having caught WhyPox. While both of them used this shared knowledge as evidence for their claims that someone near them could infect them, Aidan furthered his argument with an implicit warrant that pimples do not appear immediately after infection but would appear later—a delayed reaction. This sequence of symptoms had been discussed among the youth at the club earlier that day when everyone gathered together at the beginning of the club session. Leslie summarized for the convened club members that "you first … well … the thing [avatar] says achoo a lot, and then you start getting these pink bumps all over your face." Like epidemiologists, youth were trying to piece together the WhyPox infection mechanism: what was the order of events in WhyPox infection? Aidan/masher47 was also in one of the classes that used WhyPox as part of their science curriculum about infectious diseases. In class he had read an article in the *Whyville Times* that described symptoms from the 2002 WhyPox epidemic, including the fact that pimples first appeared on the second day of infection. From a science education perspective, it is very compelling that Aidan made the connection between something he read in class and arguments he made in the club.

One interesting phenomenon involved the spread and acceptance of the popular claim at the club that it took seven days to recover from WhyPox. Aidan/masher47 seemed to be the main source of this idea at the club. The same article where he read about the order of events of infection also put forward the idea that WhyPox only lasted for seven days in 2002 (see figure 6.4). He propagated this idea within the club, which was subsequently repeated and accepted by other members. While Aidan and others based their claim of the seven-day duration on information they read in the article, it is interesting that the reference was not necessary once this information was accepted as a fact and commonly known among the club members. In many instances, the seven-day rule was invoked readily by club members in their conversations:

Blake: Aidan, it takes you *a week* to heal?
Aidan: Yeah.

And later:

Lela: What is WhyPox?
Paolo: You only get sick if you're around sick people.
Lela: Well, I'm not around sick people.
Paolo: Good, then you're healthy.
Leslie: It's only *a week*, no big deal.
Blake: I know it does only last like *a week*.

The seven-day idea traveled like a meme from classroom into the casual conversations at the after-school club. It illustrates how a common knowledge base can form around the youth's shared activity. This shared knowledge was present in the kids' conversations as they bantered with each other and tried to convince each other of their claims about WhyPox. These youth-initiated discussions show a great deal of sophistication and illustrate the potential of informal science conversations.[13]

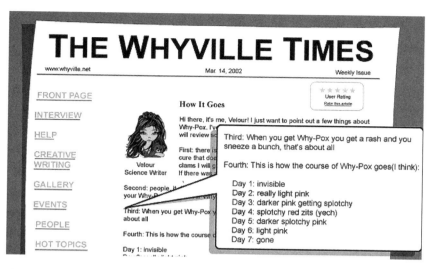

Figure 6.4
Excerpt from a *Whyville Times* article addressing WhyPox and its duration.

Focused Science Discussions in the Classroom

In contrast, discussions among students in the science classroom about WhyPox were more focused. This is not surprising since as part of science class, students participated in a curriculum designed to accompany play in Whyville.[14] Several activities were included in the curriculum:

• Going into the virtual CDC's archive in teams to read about past WhyPox infections and posted statements about possible explanations.

• Using the simulators to try out different parameter configurations (e.g., number of people infected, days of incubation, run of disease).

• Mapping the two classrooms' infection rates on a daily basis and noting the names of those who had been infected by WhyPox.

• Checking the population graph in the virtual CDC and comparing their class's infection rate with that in the community.

• Reading about previous WhyPox outbreaks in articles from the archive of the *Whyville Times*.

• Playing in Whyville during and after school hours.

We found that the students' understanding of natural infectious disease improved significantly.[15] At the beginning and end of the study, we tested students' scientific arguments by giving them a scenario about a girl who became sick the day after visiting a sick friend. Students were then asked to write about the following open-ended questions: "Why did it take a whole day for her to feel sick after the germs got inside her body?" and "How did the germs make her feel sick in so many parts of her body at the same time?" Our analyses revealed that before studying WhyPox, students responded with more prebiological answers than biological answers to both questions, but after participating in the WhyPox epidemic and accompanying curriculum, the number of biological answers increased two-fold.[16] To understand more about what students had learned about science, we also looked to their class discussions to see the kinds of theories, evidence, and observations that came into play in their arguments about WhyPox.

When talking about WhyPox, students and their teachers often used more scientific terminology than kids in the club, including words like "contagious," "exposure," "symptoms," "infection," "incubation period," "epidemiologist," "epidemic," "quarantining," or "immunity." In their conversations, teachers and students would also draw analogies and comparisons between WhyPox and real natural diseases such as SARS, the plague, or the common cold. Consider the following exchange:

Bert: I was at the [Whyville] beach and I went to someone who had them. Then I moved away.

Teacher: So you got them right away? Do you really think you got them from him? If you are around someone who has a cold and I'm around you right now will by after school I have that cold? No. Why? Because it takes a little …

Sam: It takes a little time to go through your body.

Teacher: It's called an incubation period. You're not going to get it immediately.

Susan: I got it immediately.

Teacher: So, maybe you didn't get it from him, just a suggestion.

Sam: I wanted to infect other people so I went close to them and then I went away and then they got it.

Teacher: We're going to have to talk about WhyPox ethics. [She points to the graph on the whiteboard and Post-its with names of infected students.] So the 17th? 18th?

Susan: A lot of people in this class have WhyPox.

Teacher: We have a lot more in this class. We need to be visiting—

Sam: Only those people in the other class have it.

Teacher: Interesting difference, huh? Saturday? Sunday?

Susan: I have something to say. Well, maybe a lot more people have it in here because Tony said that Theo and Sam got it first and since we're usually on the computers at the same time, maybe that we were together and we were at the same room or something.

Teacher: I'm seeing epidemiologists in all of you. You're already thinking about how did this happen, what could be the reasons, you're analyzing it, you're thinking about it. I want you to continue with that line of thought as you're looking at all of the data. Thinking why, how, what. Okay, Garth?

Garth: Well, you know how people said it was gone a few weeks ago. I think Theo got it first a long time ago, then Theo said it's gone. And it said on the news, bulletin, WhyPox has gone. But then two weeks later suddenly it's like a giant plague.

Susan: It's an epidemic.

Garth: It's the giant plague. It traveled back. It's like a WhyPlague. Now it's like everybody is getting it.

Susan: It's an epidemic.

In this extended conversation, one can see the more formally scientific discussions about WhyPox in the class. Students shared their experiences of how they caught it (Bert, Susan, Garth) or even how they tried to spread it (Sam). Post-it notes on the board mirrored the infection rate graph at the virtual CDC in Whyville, noting when each student had caught WhyPox. This display helped students compare the infection rates of the two classes—in one class many more students had caught WhyPox than in another class. This led students like Sam and Susan to *observe* from that data that there was a difference between infection rates of the classes and to *theorize* about why that might be (because more students were near each other and playing at the same time in that class over the weekend). Occasionally, the teacher introduced scientific terminology to describe what the students had observed, like "incubation period." She also called the students "epidemiologists" because of the ways that they were asking about how the epidemic was spreading, what reasons there might be for who caught it and when, and why one class seemed to be more infected than another.

Serious Science Play in Virtual Worlds

Several research studies have shown that using students' everyday observations and experiences can help them connect and think about science in their everyday lives.[17] Yet though nearly everyone experiences viruses like the common cold, the spread of viruses is not usually easy to study in a small community, because epidemics happens on a much broader scale—with people traveling around cities and countries and not just in an isolated community. WhyPox allowed us to study a large-scale epidemic in a safe manner. Kids experience the emotional investment of being infected without actually endangering their health. It also facilitated data displays that students could use on an individual, classroom, and virtual worldwide basis, seeing their individual data points in relation to many others and tracing the spread of infection across classmates and the virtual world at large. In this way, WhyPox provided personal experiences that were scientifically relevant for investigating significant issues of public health that had real-world trends. Both in the classroom but also in free online play, tweens engaged in various and sometimes sophisticated ways with the virtual outbreak, coming to understand the causes and spread of infectious disease and making connections between virtual and real infectious diseases. Virtual epidemics are just one way these types of participatory simulations can be used for learning with science games.

From our perspective, WhyPox is a type of community science game that offers a unique opportunity for designing and investigating learning opportunities in a variety of settings, from free play online, to outside-of-school settings, to within school. As a community science game, WhyPox affected all individuals in Whyville whether they were infected or saw others who were infected. The "game" provoked curiosity and shared emotional affect among players. Educational tools helped players analyze the game and predict what might happen next. Since our investigation of WhyPox, the viral epidemic has grown to include vaccinations, multiple player-designed viruses with different symptoms, and preventative care like washing hands and player-designed vaccines.

What allowed WhyPox to be successful and how might we strengthen its educational influence? First, WhyPox itself tapped into some of the most common activities and priorities of the virtual space: designing cool-looking avatars and socializing with other players.[18] It also lasted long enough for players to be curious and investigate its causes but short enough that they did not become too frustrated or bored with it. Future iterations of WhyPox granted players more active roles in avoiding or curing WhyPox. These ideas suggest the need for a matrix of key dimensions for community games: a *temporal* dimension that defines the length of the community event (from one day to several days or weeks), an *impact* dimension that is based on the core features of community life (online appearance, online discussions), and an *active choice* dimension that describes the event participation as either by choice or by presence and indicates to what degree players can intervene. A possible fourth dimension would be the *scale* of impact, whether the whole community or just a subsection is affected and whether they participate by choice or experience in the event.

The design of educational resources related to community games should also be considered. Compared to other spaces within Whyville that players frequent, the virtual CDC is heavily text-based and solitary—players cannot operate the simulations with others virtually present. This is one advantage to having classroom or club members around—they can look at computer screens together and share ideas. The virtual CDC could be redesigned so that it is similar to other locations within Whyville that allow players to see who is in the same space as them as well as allowing for chatting so that groups of friends are able to investigate WhyPox together. Such social interaction within the virtual CDC could leverage players' sense of community within Whyville. New elements to the WhyPox epidemic could also allow players to intervene in the epidemic, increasing players' agency and potentially encouraging deeper investigations into WhyPox, because those investigations can have a real effect on how the epidemic plays out.

Whyville features other examples of community science games such as the Red Tide, Kinematic Attic, and WhyPower. Each of these activities involves phenomena that have affected Whyville in a community-wide way. For instance, the Red Tide initially appeared in 2007 at the popular Whyville hangouts at the beach at the same time as the coast of southern Florida experienced a Red Tide alert in 2007. The beach turned red, and Whyvillians visited a beach house to learn how to resolve the Red Tide. They collected samples of water, analyzed them in a laboratory to find out what caused the ecological disaster, then used sensors to find the highest concentrations of select pollutants near the coast where they paid (!) to plant seedlings to alleviate the problem. Other community games have involved Whyvillians in studying what allows some avatars to move faster than others and how to reduce pollutants from various power sources. We see these community games in free-play virtual environments as vast, largely unstudied opportunities for kids to investigate and experience science in engaging ways. They also provide powerful ways for creating new kinds of daily shared experiences that can productively connect learning inside and outside classrooms. Then, during the next outbreak of WhyPox, those Whyvillians who will experience the epidemic anew could be coupled with those players who are more experienced who in turn could have opportunities to impart their own uniquely earned science-based wisdom.

In fact, not only science educators but also epidemiologists have seen the potential of virtual epidemics for learning. In 2007, Eric Lofgren and

Nina Fefferman published a report in *Lancet Infectious Diseases* about what epidemiologists could learn from the Corrupted Blood outbreak in the popular virtual game World of Warcraft.[19] The virulent, contagious disease was introduced by maker Blizzard Entertainment as an extra challenge to high-level players. But, just as a real virus might spread, the disease was accidentally carried out of its intended containment area within the game and thousands of players ended up dying, creating a full blown epidemic that allowed scientists a rare opportunity to study human behavior in such a circumstance. Some avatars fled their infected counterparts, others attacked them, and still others—in a mix of empathy and curiosity—came to their rescue, thus infecting themselves and heightening the epidemic. Lofgren and Fefferman discovered that Warcraft players demonstrated empathy and curiosity, behaviors that had not previously been included in mathematicians' models to make predictions about human actions in an epidemic outbreak. Despite the entirely "virtual" nature of the situation, behaviors displayed in play very much offer a point of consideration for those interested in likewise understanding human behavior in the "real world."[20]

One of Whyville's strengths as an informal virtual science world is that it is free and available to anyone, anytime. This is also a challenge to using it in more formal educational settings. Timing was a key aspect of our integration of virtual epidemics in the science curriculum of two classrooms, arguably the areas where the most science learning occurred. We were able to schedule the outbreak of WhyPox when the unit took place because this was a research project. Other educational virtual worlds have more structured approaches and are meant to be used primarily in *classrooms* rather than in free play. For instance, in the virtual worlds of RiverCity[21] designed by Harvard researcher Chris Dede along with Brian Nelson and Diane Ketelhut, players traveled back in time to investigate epidemic outbreaks in a fictive nineteenth-century environment rather than directly experiencing an epidemic in real time. Students collected data samples at different locations, generated hypotheses, tested these in parallel with each other, and developed recommendations for improving living conditions and sanitary systems. The design of a similar virtual world, Quest Atlantis,[22] led by Arizona State University researcher Sasha Barab, also employs quests where students work in teams to solve problems like environmental contamination in their virtual world. Both of these virtual worlds have been successfully implemented in science classes and demonstrated not only academic but also motivational benefits to students. These are by no means the only examples of virtual worlds for learning, but they have been studied more extensively and provide a better sense of how to realize the potential of virtual worlds for both research and education that Bainbridge (2007) pointed to in his *Science* article. Community games provide opportunities for kids to investigate and experience science in engaging ways. They also provide powerful ways to create new kinds of daily shared experiences that can connect learning inside and outside classrooms in productive manners.

7 Designing Connected Play

So there you go, a step-by-step to becoming a Whyville designer. It will be frustrating at first, because drawing on a computer screen with a mouse can be very tricky, but you'll get used to it with practice. Only time can bring out your skills. And don't worry if you aren't much of an artist in real life; Whyville can be a good place for you to begin to practice your skills. Anybody can draw if they want to, they just need to spend the time training their eye to recognize things like proportion and modeling without much thinking. It takes longer for some people than others, but everyone can do it, even you. So don't ever get discouraged and give up, you could be the next biggest Whyville designer next year!
—Twigsy, "So You Want to Be a Designer?"[1]

We started our examination of connected play with the premise that it is play within a designed space. Virtual worlds such as Whyville are designed spaces: companies host virtual worlds on a server, configuring the space for content and activities, while players populate these virtual worlds by interacting with each other and contributing content in various ways. In Whyville, design is an intentional, even invited part of everyday play. We have already discussed the intricate ways in which players design their avatars using face parts created by other players. The article written by Twigsy quoted above provides step-by-step instructions on how you can become a face-part designer,[2] concluding with the challenges and possible recognition awaiting prospective designers.

This chapter focuses on the design of virtual worlds—how different dimensions of these spaces can be designed to support connected play. The design space of virtual worlds is a vast and complicated enterprise with many dimensions.[3] Like educational designer Marina Bers, we understand virtual worlds as designed spaces that can either constrain or open up opportunities for intentional personal, social, and educational development.[4] Further, design happens on multiple levels, including designing *for* players and designing *by* players. Indeed, in this chapter we further consider designing for player-generated designs: how to create design opportunities for players in different ways and in spaces both inside and outside virtual worlds. We especially focus on the affordances that constructive activities for players have to offer for connected play. For that, we build on activities around identity and cheats that we have found to be key in connected play. In the following sections, we examine two cases in more detail: *identity play*, which leverages players' intense engagement with avatar designs and builds on our insights from chapter 3, and *boundary play*, which leverages community practices of cheating. We examine a case study of how a collective of Whyville players worked on developing a cheat to a new science game that provides a compelling illustration of how cheating (discussed in chapter 5) can be leveraged in productive ways for learning.

Designing for Identity Play

One of the common challenges faced in the field of learning with video games and virtual worlds is helping kids to critique the designs and cultures of the in-game worlds they learn to inhabit. Kids are quite adept at learning the values and culture of the worlds in which they play (for instance, learning how to look good in Whyville). Yet it is much more difficult to help kids to see beyond the game, to recognize that games and virtual worlds are designed by people and therefore are not be perfect and can be changed.[5] In Whyville, this becomes more complex, as players contribute significantly to designs on the site, especially in regard to avatar parts and social interactions. Thus, tweens are in many ways the designers and social drivers of appearance in Whyville, with the implicit challenge that they often do not critique the society that they help to create. For instance, although many Whyvillians complain about how they were made fun of when they dressed as newbies (see chapter 3), as soon as they reach greater competence in dressing they often begin to make fun of others as well. To disrupt this tendency and to promote deeper creativity in avatar design, we created a week-long costume contest in our 2008 after-school club.

We started the "costume contest" midway through the club, just when club members had moved past their newbie looks and established recognizable, customized looks on Whyville. The challenge was for the youth and adults to see who could come up with the "most different" look from what they had had before. Though the members were reluctant to change the looks that had finally allowed them to set aside their newbie status, members made some very creative designs: two boys became girls (Ben and Sam), two women mentors became boys, one boy (Tyrone) moved from a newbie to an anime look, one girl (Taylor) moved from a put-together look to a collage of random face parts, and another girl (Lucetta) became a bald, green-faced alien with old lady clothes (figure 7.1 shows contest pictures of Ben, Tyrone, and Taylor before and after our contest). One can easily see the significant differences in how they looked before and during the contest.

Ben

Tyrone

Taylor

Figure 7.1
Before (left) and after (right) costume contest pictures.

After the contest ended, we solicited reflections on how the changes in their looks affected how other Whyvillians responded to them. Everyone explained the ways that their new look changed how others interacted with them. Some gained popularity, others ridicule. Ben felt very uncomfortable as a girl because girls came up to him and started talking to him about "girl things" like "what's in your purse?" In contrast, with his new anime look, Tyrone was on the receiving end of many new flirtations and also started to make some friends with similar interests in his favorite anime series. Taylor experienced mixed reactions to her change in looks, in part because her costume contest look was very different from Whyville standards. As a result, many people treated her as though she were new and inexperienced:

Deborah: So how did it feel when, uh, people interacted with you differently?
Taylor: Well, it was sorta weird, but cool at the same time, 'cause like, you um, met more people and stuff, like, uh other times they would just be like "get away from me."

On the one hand, many greeted and talked with her in a friendly way; on the other hand, many dismissed her as ugly and told her to "get away." Lucetta's costume contest experience stood out strongly because of the intentionality with which she created an ugly avatar on Whyville: a green, snarling alien. All of her choices were by design: picking the green alien head, choosing a scary mouth, and deciding on an "old lady" outfit and adding a hat for contrast, "'cause [her avatar] was so bald ... Women don't like to be bald." In her alien design she juxtaposed feminine features (the "old lady" dress, the wide-brimmed hat) with the snarling green alien. She purposefully chose these qualities to be original, "different than all the rest of them," and the pictures in figure 7.2 demonstrate how different her avatar looks were, even though they both involved purposeful, thematic choices that reflected her priority on fashion and her sense of what was attractive in Whyville. One look was attuned to what was beautiful in Whyville, and one daringly reflected what was ugly there.

Lucetta's alien avatar certainly influenced how others treated her in Whyville. She reflected afterward:

Lucetta: It was odd. A lot of people were—some people were mean.
Deborah: Oh, like how?
Lucetta: Like I would go over and they'd um, some person went "555 if she's ugly," and there's this whole bunch of people saying "555. 555." Then I'm like "Thank you!" [perks up with high tone] ... Then they probably were surprised when I said "thank you."

Lucetta

Figure 7.2a–g
Lucetta before and during the costume contest.

After describing how others called her ugly and treated her meanly, Lucetta went on to say that one Whyvillian befriended her during that time period, but even then, he and others were more friendly when she reverted to her earlier look. Other club members also reflected on how their avatar designs changed during the contest and how others treated them differently. Tyrone assembled a variety of face parts from different Japanese anime characters and found that some Whyvillians began to initiate conversations with him about a shared interest in particular manga. Taylor chose to put a mass assemblage of fun face parts together on her face and found that this caused others to interpret her as a newbie and to refuse to talk to her. After the contest, all but Tyrone happily went back to more traditional looks.

We hosted the contest for two reasons. First, we hoped to encourage reflection on how people often judge others by their looks. As noted, many Whyvillians who were once ridiculed because of their "newbie" appearance take up these same denigrative practices as soon as they become recognized insiders in Whyville, something that happened in our first after-school club. The costume contest helped kids reflect on the ways people treated them differently when they altered their avatars. Second, this contest was an attempt to stimulate youth to experiment creatively with some of the design opportunities in making avatars while reflecting on the social responses this generated. Boellstorff has noted how many individuals do not take advantage of the great freedom of the avatar design tools in Second

Life, most often mirroring their own physical appearance and responding to the social norms on the site.[6] We designed the contest to disrupt this social pattern and encourage kids to be creative when establishing their identity in a virtual space.

Designing for Boundary Play

Now we turn our attention to rethinking the cheating that is so prevalent in many virtual worlds and video games by focusing on constructive aspects of these practices. Although much attention is often spent on ethical challenges associated with boundary play, the practice of developing cheats has a silver lining that is rarely discussed. In many environments, cheat sites are thought to detract from the game. Here we describe how a Whyville member built his own cheat site for Whyville, but rather than detracting from Whyville it embodied Whyville's principles and actually supported people's enjoyment and participation in the site.

We present a case study of a collective cheat development we call GameSite.net, one of the prominent Whyville cheat sites hosted unofficially outside of the game, that provides an informative illustration of how player-designed cheats can contribute to learning and engagement. GameSite .net was a Whyville cheat site with the most extensive listing of cheats, including Easter eggs, cheat codes, game guides, walkthroughs, and work-arounds. The site was created by a Whyvillian in mid-2004 and, according to the history posted on the site, underwent several designs until in mid-2006 it began becoming quite popular with thirty-four registered users and two hundred visitors a day on average.[7] The site's owner and designer, a fourteen-year-old boy in 2006, and his three administrators actively contributed to and monitored participation on the site, posting new messages on the home page of the site roughly four times a month, not including numerous responses to messages on the forums. On the home page, the site designer wrote regular updates about progress in developing cheats for new games in addition to general tips on becoming an insider in Whyville. Other Whyville players posted comments about cheats they had figured out in a game, pleas for more or better cheats, and praise for the help offered on the site. While the site designer and his site administrators officially managed and posted the cheats, the activity of gathering and synthesizing the cheats was a collaborative effort, and the leaders gave credit to those who had assisted with various parts of researching and developing the cheats.

During our observation of the site, a new game, called the Spitzer Spectrometer (see figure 7.3), appeared in Whyville. Players encountered a great deal of difficulty in winning the game. At the core, Spitzer Spectrometer was a timed memory game where players matched images from a spectrometer to their respective elements. A spectrometer is a scientific instrument that measures the brightness of different wavelengths of light. In Whyville, the game used a kind of spectrometer where materials are heated to the point at which they emit light, which is passed through a diffraction grating that spreads out the light as a rainbow. Each element has a unique spectral signature, like a fingerprint. The output of this spectrometer appears as colored bars, like individually separated lines of color. By studying the bars of light in the spectrum emitted by a particular material, scientists can identify what element(s) the material is made of. This is primarily how astronomers identify what elements are present in distant stars and how chemists identify elements in various compounds.

In the first level of the game, players had 120 seconds to match five elements to their individual spectral images. A spectral image appeared at the top of the page. The player had to guess which element made that image, testing elements one by one by dragging an element either to the Bunsen burner (for solid elements) or to a gas discharge lamp (for gaseous elements). When the light from a heated element hit the spectrometer, the element's spectrum appeared below the picture of the spectrum to match. If they selected the correct element they got a match. Players needed five matches for each level. At the second level, the game became more difficult as players had to match more complex spectra emitted from compounds containing two elements, not just one. Figure 7.3 displays the successful matching of the spectra of two elements to the image.

Although the Spitzer Spectrometer is a basic matching game, the time limit of 120 seconds for five matches was overwhelming not only for one of the authors who was previously familiar with spectroscopy but apparently also for many other players who posted urgent requests for the cheat site to finish the cheat. One of the main problems was that the lines of the spectra were not easy to memorize, so the main tactic of playing the game—methodically trying out each element one by one for each new spectrum to be matched—was not efficient enough to meet the time limit.

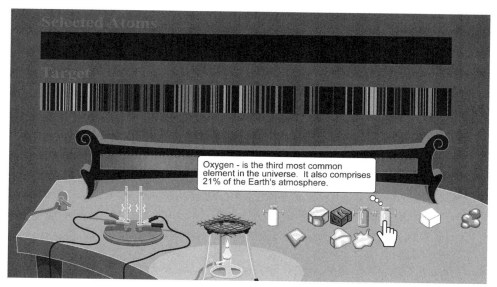

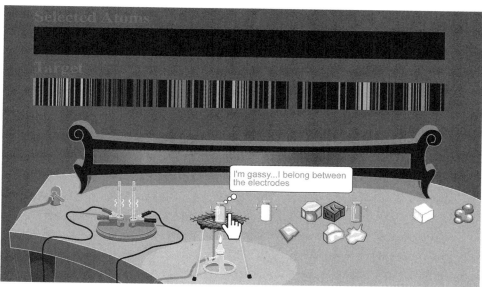

Figure 7.3
Spitzer Spectrometer, level 2.

Encountering these difficulties, the cheat site developers did some research on the game and then made a more general plea for help on the site's main forum:

August 13, 2006:

This new game (Spitzer Spectrometer) is to hard for us to figure out. We have read up on Spectroscpoy on the internet and found nothing on it! Now since we can't figure the game out we need your help to give us the answers so we can give them to every one else. We will give the first person who respondes to us with the correct answers 2000 clams! If you give it to use in the nexted 48 hours (2 days) it will be 3000 clams, but after that it will be 2000.

The offer of 2,000 to 3,000 clams represented over two weeks' accumulated salary (130 clams was the upper limit of a daily salary on Whyville) and was a generous reward. It seems even greater when one considers that the site owner would gain only a few clams by increasing his salary through completing the game (maximally eight clams a day if he completed all four levels). Thus, the motivation for designing a cheat seems to be to serve the community with knowledge and to figure out the game. A few days later, still with no success, the site owner posted that he was going on vacation, and a grass-roots effort to figure out the game began in earnest. There were many frustrated postings on the site by Whyvillians discouraged in their efforts to play the game. Finally, one week after the original plea a girl came up with a clever solution, posted her solution online, and told the forum about her cheat:

August 20, 2006:

I made somewhat of a cheat. ... Well its just all the elements names with the colors they make on the spectrum ... [lists website]. It looks better before I upload it ... haha.

—Site Participant

The cheat consisted of individual screenshots taken of each element's spectrum and listed as a table (see figure 7.4), what one might consider a scientific reference guide similar to what professional scientists might use to discern which element's spectrum they are observing.

Within a day, a different cheat site designer who also participated on GameSite.net posted this girl's cheat on his own site and directed GameSite.net participants to it so they could find it more easily (giving full credit to the username of the girl who created the cheat). One day after that, he

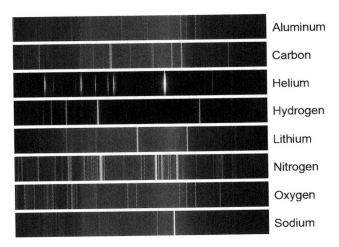

Aluminum

Carbon

Helium

Hydrogen

Lithium

Nitrogen

Oxygen

Sodium

Figure 7.4
Reproduction of Spectrometer Cheat (Reference Guide).

made his own plea on GameSite.net's forum for more people to join in fig-uring out a cheat for the higher levels of the game:

August 22, 2006:

We gotta get some answers quick! I am going to form a group of people to work dif-ferent solutions out for spitzer spectrometer. All we are doing is in our spare time, we will experiment with the game and see what we can do with it. Especially level 2. Level 2 is nothing but trouble for everyone. So i hope to get answers as soon as possible. Remember everyone reading, if you have answers SUBMITT them. It will benifit us all. ...

—Site Participant/Outside Cheat Site Designer

Finally, when GameSite.net's designer returned from vacation, he put the girl's cheat on the main cheat page with full credit and told the com-munity about this on the home page. The cheat itself would be classified as a "guide" on our typology (see table 5.1). It changed the game strategy from one of trial and error to a more systematic and less time-consuming search by providing a reference table of the spectra of all the elements. Indeed, the strategy was quite scientific.

Beyond just furnishing cheats for salary-raising games, GameSite.net pro-vided cultural hints for participating in Whyville (where to hang out, how to make friends, where to shop for the best face parts), additional cheats not intrinsic to monetary success in Whyville (how to ride in a virtual car without a seatbelt, a computer code for throwing projectiles faster), and a space to discuss appropriate behavior on the forum. For instance, though answers to the chat license test (the test all Whyvillians must pass in order to be able to chat in Whyville) were posted, the cheat included a warning that one should understand the reasons for the answers and not just use the cheats without considering their meaning.[8]

It was also interesting that the cheat site owner enforced many of Whyville's own rules and conventions on his site. For example, he closely watched forum postings for inappropriate material and advertising of other sites: "every one who swears a lot, spams, or cusses ... will be banned." Looking through the forum, one can see many times when messages or parts of them have been blocked or erased by the owner. In addition, other forum participants pointed out what they saw as rude comments left on the site. For instance, when one user complained that there were not enough cheats or that the site did not help him enough, another user replied that the site owner did a lot of work on others' behalf and that they should all be grateful for the help he provided. Finally, while the site recognized that scams occurred, it did not support them and purposefully tried to distance itself from that practice. So while GameSite.net wholeheartedly embraced many types of cheating, including Easter eggs, cheat codes, walkthroughs, and workarounds, it did not embrace "true cheating" or spoilsport hacking that infringed on others' virtual property or identities, like Zoe's scamming to obtain clams. Beyond purely altruistic motives, hosting a cheat site as a designer and knowing about good cheat sites as a player provide a type of "gaming capital,"[9] something that gives one advantages in game play.

This Spitzer Spectrometer cheat site is a striking example of a fourteen-year-old boy leading tens, if not hundreds, of others in creating a knowledge-sharing site for members of Whyville. One irony of this cheat site is the extent to which participants created new knowledge and shared it with peers, and did so in a manner comparable to some of the best examples exhibited by communities of adults. In this regard, it is interesting that players had to leave the site of Whyville in order to have this conversation about spectrometers and how to complete the game. Although Whyville provides official forums for certain conversations, including those about community science games like Red Tide and WhyPox (see chapter 6), there is little room for knowledge building about the single player salary-raising science games like the Spitzer Spectrometer. Later in this chapter we suggest ways to make these constructive conversations possible in formal learning environments like classrooms.

Also of note, the cheat site owner and others members of the site reflected on their own values as well as the values of Whyville. They took responsibility for managing comments on the forums, deciding which cheats to post, and differentiating between cheats in the spirit of making a salary or finishing a game versus cheats that harmed others outright. This is but one of many examples of the ways that Whyvillians' sense of morality was lived out not only in Whyville but also in other online communities.

Designing for Connected Play

These two examples illustrate how constructive activities can become part of connected play. A small change of viewpoint can help us rethink these activities in terms of designing for connected spaces. Each type of play discussed above resulted from connections between one space outside of Whyville and Whyville itself. Our costume contest made connections between an after-school club and Whyville. The cheat site connected players from Whyville to another virtual site where they shared and built knowledge. This provides an interesting way to think about educational opportunities in virtual worlds by designing for connections with other everyday settings that tweens occupy. Below we return to these two examples to think through intentional designs for connective play.

After-School Clubs and Shared Play Spaces

Our costume contest drew together two spaces—an after-school club and Whyville—to encourage reflection on an important everyday value, namely, respect for others regardless of appearance. The contest was a designed intervention developed to stimulate innovation in players' own created looks and to make connections to values they had been taught at home and in school. After all, Whyville and other virtual worlds are not the only places where kids make fun of people who look different or who self-consciously tailor their looks in order to fit in. But Whyville provided a relatively safe and easy place to play with remaking one's look. Where else can one so easily change skin color, facial features, or become an alien?

There are many other ways to build on kids' shared online playing experiences to stimulate reflection on important values and everyday activities, not just with identity or appearance but also with other practices such as being kind to strangers, confronting bullies, and practicing what to say to find common interests with potential friends. The key is recognizing challenges and opportunities in the virtual world—common values, problematic practices, creative openings—and making a playful experience that capitalizes on the special circumstances in the overlapping space between a club or other shared play space and a virtual world. Open-ended constructive activities in a virtual world are one key place to look for opportunities for designing connected play.[10]

Classrooms and Knowledge Construction

Educators ask us regularly how to take advantage of the opportunities in virtual worlds and other kinds of educational technology to influence student learning. WhyPox provides one example—taking advantage of something that can be simulated only in a massive setting (like an epidemic) and using kids' Whyville experiences to build individual and collective knowledge about related topics important in education. This seems particularly relevant with topics that require large amounts of data or many people, like epidemics or statistics. Cheating offers a second kind of opportunity—learning by designing cheats. We can think of this as transgressive design, extending learning activities by asking players to become designers of cheat sites as a way to engage in science, ethics, and technology.

When cheating becomes a community practice of building and sharing knowledge rather than an individual act, cheating becomes part of learning. This also means that learners can benefit from being involved in new forms of participation like the ones we observed around designing cheat sites and participating in discussions. We propose transgressive design as a way of moving from cheating practices to cheating designs, shifting our focus from seeing players as consumers to seeing them as constructive designers of cheats and cheat sites. We found that the designs and interactions on cheat sites reveal a great deal about the designers' understanding of the community and associated practices. Cheat-site participants are invested in Whyville, in promoting others' success in Whyville, and in displaying their knowledge of Whyville. Like most Whyvillians, cheat-site participants view the object of the game as participating in the larger Whyvillian culture—salary-raising games like the Spitzer Spectrometer are mostly a means to a greater end. In fact, cheat-site participants of

GameSite.net also valued the morals of Whyville, as displayed in qualifiers to their chat cheats, which asked viewers to read carefully and understand the principles behind the questions.[11] Further, they took the time to learn the inside secrets of Whyville, and often did substantial research to develop their sites and learn how to complete the science games.

How might educators encourage cheating design as a type of constructive practice in classrooms? One way might be to encourage learners to develop and share their own cheats for games in a virtual world. The better the game, the more likely the cheat will help players understand aspects of science or practices of research—like making a reference guide for spectra of common elements. Taking this a step further, we might ask our students to brainstorm ways to "cheat" in our own classes. One of us did that with her own graduate course, asking her students to form small groups and figure out "how you would cheat in this class, within the spirit of learning." Of course this might not always be an applicable idea, but imagine if students shared reading strategies (as they did in the author's class), highlighted main ideas, or developed new visualizations to help in understanding key issues. We might also use this to evaluate the designs of our own classes—if students "cheated" the class, would that result in learning some of the key ideas or practices of the course or would it only bypass the learning needed for the course?

Constructive Affinity Sites

The examples discussed here provide just one illustration of how constructive activities can expand connected play. From observations in other social networking forums such as the substantial Minecraft and Scratch communities, it is clear that one major attraction of constructive activities is building relationships connected to shared affinities. Minecraft, with over 16 million members,[12] lets players create objects and buildings using textured 3D blocks to design their own immersive environments. The virtual world of Minecraft provides a rough template with different biozones, runs through a night and day cycle, and is populated with nonplayer characters. Different modes of game play are possible, including exploring, in which players can travel to different parts of the world; crafting, in which players can build and share objects to use in the world; and combat, in which players are required to maintain health and shelter in order to survive attacks from hostile players and creatures. In particular, the crafting modes of Minecraft offer potential learning benefits. For instance, some players have used the physics engine to build simple systems ranging from mechanical devices to electric circuits and more complex systems such as CPUs. Much like the virtual trading post in Whyville, many Minecraft members also design and share their created objects.

Another social networking forum is centered around Scratch, a media-rich programming language that allows youth to design, share, and remix software programs in the form of games, stories, and animations.[13] Since its public launch in May 2007, the Scratch website has provided a place for users to share their work with one another. With over 700,000 registered contributors and over 2.8 million projects shared to date, the Scratch website is a vibrant online community where over 1,000 new projects are uploaded every day. It is possible to use Scratch as an individual programming tool or in traditional small-group formats, but the website also facilitates broader types of collaboration including open-source sharing and remixing of posted projects. Kids can share their own projects, download projects, comment on others' projects, curate galleries of projects (their own and others'), and ask questions on the forums. Scratch activities take place online but often connect to after-school clubs,[14] classes,[15] and community centers[16] where kids use Scratch to design game software, music videos, animations, and many other projects.

This is just a small selection of many examples where connected play expands into constructive play. Developing shared productions illustrates the next level of membership and commitment in virtual communities—much like Twigsy described in her article, "So You Want to Be a Designer?," here is where we see connected play develop into richer forms of participation that focus on shared interests and contributions. Such activities, already present in Whyville, deserve a larger presence in virtual worlds.

8 Future Play

In this book about tween play in a virtual world, we set out to reimagine play in the digital publics of today's world. Our motivations were simple—to understand what kids do in virtual worlds and how that matters for their play. Play is a fundamentally important activity for tweens, especially as they transition from childhood into adolescence. We traveled a number of paths as we traced tweens' play and its meanings across their social worlds, avatar designs, identities, relationships of all kinds, boundaries, ethics, and even epidemics. Above all, our argument has been that play in digital publics is connected. Relationships, values, identities—even tweens' social and psychological development—fuse across their play in and beyond virtual worlds.

Let's return for a moment to Zoe and her avatar bluwave[1] and review what we've learned about her as she played in the world of Whyville. Creating her avatar involved hard work finding racially appropriate face parts, learning about the different places where she could get them, and assembling them into an appropriate online representation. In the process, issues of race, gender, and representation were as much present as they were in her everyday life. Perhaps the constellations were a bit different, but her experiences nevertheless capture many of the challenges that tweens face as they strive to fit in while tailoring their representations to their unique needs and desires.

We also learned that getting to know others was not just a matter of hanging out. Creating a viable and attractive online persona was a first step, but Zoe had to search out contacts, as evidenced by her numerous attempts to meet and get to know others. Not surprisingly, she often chose to meet and play with others from the club online. As evidenced by Zoe's exchanges, learning to play with others in the digital public requires as much social navigation as it does in the offline world. Along the way, she also encountered other challenges when another player scammed her and she in turn started scamming others. Only virtual clams were lost, but Zoe's distress was palpable when she realized what had happened and tried to alert others about the perpetrators. For Zoe, it was a harsh lesson—one we surely wish hadn't happened to her or any other player. What do we make out of her temporary career move of becoming a scammer? Is it mitigated by the fact that it was temporary? That many of her peers engaged in it as well? It surely raises important and critical questions of what good and responsible play means and how kids learn about it.

The claim we've made in this book is that understanding Zoe's participation in the digital public required understanding and connecting all of her play, not just the avatar design which was visible and she chose to be more open about, but also the flirting and scamming which she chose to be silent about perhaps because she feared social ramifications by adults and peers. The rampant flirting attempts and her scamming experiences, both as a victim and perpetrator, skidded at the boundary of acceptable. Along the way, she became a skilled Whyville member and chose to extend her play to home, friends, and others, long beyond the official run of the after-school club. Being on Whyville was a meaningful experience that connected to her interests, needs, and desires (despite some of the challenges), in ways we described and others we may not know of. Understanding connected play like Zoe's and that of her peers was one agenda that we pursued with this work, because digital publics are spaces visited by millions of kids but largely ignored in conversations about digital media and learning, especially those publics created for children and tweens.[2]

Understanding Connected Play

Understanding connected play in digital publics stands on its own in contributing to the larger body of work on children's play. Many scholars have documented the practices of children's play across cultures and centuries.[3] We hope that our efforts contribute a small but significant portion to documenting children's play in virtual worlds. Understanding the practices of children's play is important for understanding their development and learning, and also for understanding the values of the cultures in which children are growing up.

Reimagining Play

We began by documenting the minutiae that consume so much of every-day life online just as they do offline. Understanding the ordinary in a seemingly extraordinary environment allowed us to uncover the social fabric of tweens' play in Whyville, from their daily shopping trips to earning money from science games to networking with others in the virtual world. We saw how their language changed, their looks developed, and their social games progressed as they became full-fledged members of the virtual community—virtual only by status of being based online, not because it was intangible or ethereal. Studying the very mundaneness of their daily activities allowed us to uncover the challenges of learning to participate in a new culture, the dominant values that shape that culture, and the regular practices of that culture. Against this backdrop, some actions stood out as significant when individuals pressed back against the design, values, and practices of the virtual world in innovative, and at times problematic, ways that allowed them to connect aspects of who they were elsewhere while still being legitimate members of their virtual community.

Indeed, when play was *not* connected is when play became problematic. Instances of such disconnectedness include racial disparities in face-part availability, preventing some Whyvillians like Zoe from making avatars that reflected their real-life skin color, or the commodification of other players through scamming them or accumulating them for the sake of amplifying one's total number of boyfriends and/or girlfriends. Against these disconnections we see innovations in tweens' play that stand out: when Zoe and Briana made new avatars (Latina and Pixie) that were attractive *and* went against the normative "whiteness" on Whyville, when cheating became a collaborative knowledge-building activity that helped many players succeed in science games, when members of the club used Whyville to extend their friendships beyond the space of school, and when Whyvillians writing in the *Whyville Times* pressed for new attitudes toward flirting as well as design changes regarding avatars and race. All of these instances, as well as others, increased the potential for making more rich and meaningful connections online. Both the mundane and the problematic were needed to understand where play was connected, and where it was not.

Play in the digital publics means both confirmation of and experimentation with cultural norms and practices for tweens. It's about fitting in and belonging *and* about pushing back and being different at the same time.

Scholars like Barrie Thorne[4] have observed how tweens negotiate tensions about gender identity through conformity seeking and boundary crossing. More poignantly, the title of Thorne's (1993) book, *"Gender Play,"* emphasizes the performative nature of interactions that take place in classrooms, hallways, and schoolyards. We see this performative nature of play in virtual worlds too, which extend public play spaces into the digital realm, expanding spaces of play and allowing new forms of play. Yet in large part, norms and practices that define play in the offline world still define and connect with play in online worlds. If there is one difference, it is how play is designed or engineered for kids[5] more than ever before. Virtual worlds are made by designers and often highly shaped by players. Reimagining play in digital publics, then, is about understanding the affordances that make room for responsible and creative play, a point we will discuss in more detail below.[6] First, though, we call for a richer understanding of play across a variety of digital publics and over time.

Rich Play

Coming to understand tween play required us to connect many different dots on the data landscape. The commercial and educational sectors have a great interest in understanding participation in these massive communities. Most certainly, commercial companies collect all kinds of information about what kids do online in virtual worlds and other apps for the purposes of increasing participation, advertising revenue, and product sales.[7] Researchers also are eager to accumulate massive amounts of data for the purposes of collecting information about participants' learning processes, in order to provide feedback and assistance for improving the design of the site. And yet, the survey studies, experimental work, and ethnographic research reports that provide rich accounts and details of individual and group participation are far and few between, especially for younger players.[8] Further, most research does not take careful account of both kids' participation in digital publics as well as their friendships, relationships with family members, and school activities. Rich play means making connections between different methodologies of research and different spaces and relationships in kids' lives.

We approached this task from both ends, leveraging massive amounts of data while also generating detailed ethnographic case studies in combination with studying community views. Any of these approaches alone provides valuable information, but they show only slices of the online experience. Where do we see the benefits of big data in what we have learned? Understanding patterns and trends in participation over large numbers of people and over extended periods of time provided a bird's-eye perspective that is difficult to obtain while standing on the ground amid hundreds and thousands of participants. Where do we see the benefits of small data? The ethnographic approach gave us a lens through which to study the norms and practices that shape play in Whyville, what it means to look cool, how to talk, and what to do. It also revealed changes in individual tweens' play over time with hints at reasons for those changes. Notably, we used big data to complete our ethnographic analyses, which added depth and richness to the study and also uncovered some hidden activities of tweens participating in the club.

The combined and integrated analyses revealed what we might have missed, had we looked in only one direction. We combined big and small data in making sense of what online life in Whyville is all about. Our insights were not gained just by following particular participants through Whyville or just by running big data analyses, but by combining big and small data in recreating life online which revealed surprising activities such as scamming and flirting, often not visible to online observers.[9] Considerable work and effort went into building these cases. The work involved knowing what big data points meant, but it also involved filling in small gaps that existed by bringing in observations from other sources and other places. Taken together and by putting it into the context of the community's activities at large, we were able to create rich, thick descriptions of what Zoe and other players did and experienced.[10] Such rich views of connected play are still rare, partially because of access issues to the backend data of virtual worlds, but also because they run against the grain of established approaches falsely dichotomized in either the qualitative or quantitative side. We connected both together and further extended our research to take into account multiple spaces of play in Whyville and beyond to generate a rich understanding of connected play in digital publics that in turn can provide a platform for designing for connected play and learning.

We see our work as a starting point for much-needed studies on the social networking forums of younger kids.[11] We need to understand where and how tweens do their "hanging out, messing around, and geeking out" in virtual worlds, as the multisite ethnography by Mizuko Ito and colleagues documented for older teens.[12] We saw the full spectrum of these activities in and around Whyville, but we also know that this is just one of the many virtual sites visited by tweens. More research is needed that captures how tweens coordinate their travels between digital publics and how they transition into new spaces as they or their friends move on to other venues.[13] Such migrations are a part of growing up and moving out into larger worlds, but little is known about what this means for digital publics. Only when we know about this will we be able to understand what "growing up digital" actually means and how play is configured in digital publics. In doing so, we must be careful to bring multiple perspectives to bear, not just our own as adults, parents, researchers, and educators, but also those of the players themselves. Understanding social practices and norms that govern play online and what kind of resources kids need to bring to play online can lead us to designing better opportunities for learning.

Designing Connected Play

In choosing Whyville as a platform for our study, we selected a virtual world that offers more freedom and creative expression than is found in most commercial worlds for children and tweens.[14] The design of personal avatars was one example where players could choose from over 30,000 parts created by other players. The inclusion of various learning games and simulations was also a unique feature. Another example was the ability to chat broadly with other players with only limited chat filters, even whispers and private email (ymail). These opportunities also represent challenges to players as they are growing up and taking on more responsibilities. All of these features, and many more, showcase the possibilities to design virtual worlds where kids not only enjoy spending their time but also are engaged in learning.

Responsible Play

One of the themes of this book has been to highlight tweens' initiative in developing appropriate responses to challenging circumstances, whether it be addressing racial inequities, the threat of scamming, or inappropriate comments. It can be challenging in a place like Whyville, which is populated primarily by tweens, to achieve an appropriate balance between protective regulation and a framework that allows for some independence and self-governance. We found many opportunities for tweens in Whyville, including friendships, games, and creative design. But we also found challenges, when play is hurtful, perhaps not in a physical sense but most definitely in a psychological sense. When Marjorie Goodwin wrote about the hidden life of girls,[15] she provided compelling evidence that girls' play comes with its own cruelties and exclusions, carefully orchestrated with words rather than blows. Responsible play is not necessarily safe, but it is foundational to learning values and responsibility.

One solution, adopted by many commercial companies, is to limit and control player behavior with technical solutions. For instance, software protocols such as pull-down menus with preselected phrases and built-in safeties such as chat filters aim to prevent certain words and behaviors. Community management, where community norms of behavior are established and maintained largely by the players themselves, is rare. Whyville stands out among many sites designed for tweens in providing players with much responsibility for managing their own behavior and reporting problematic behavior to others.[16] Indeed, when we talk about community management in virtual worlds we are actually talking about a range of choices, from worlds where the power rests firmly with the parent company's master programmers (a strong adult presence) to idealized worlds where everything is player-run. Along this continuum, we can discuss various aspects of community management in virtual worlds and the degree to which players should have control of and access to their in-game environment.

In Whyville, we found a compelling mix of company oversight and community management that seemed to work well for the mainly tween population. Transgressions certainly do occur, but a consensus seems to have emerged about which transgressions are typical and can largely be handled by players on their own and which are not. Chat filters are constantly updated and at the same time circumvented by tweens in ingenious ways, not to mention that many tweens know how to use alternative chat channels that render moot the purpose of any chat filter. There is clear adult oversight in what gets published in the online newspaper.[17] All the articles in the *Whyville Times* are written and submitted by players, screened for content, and lightly edited by an adult employee of the company that owns Whyville. The editors allow grammatical and spelling errors in keeping with the tone and transparency of tweens' writing. At the same time, the fact that the adult editor of the *Whyville Times* published articles about controversial topics such as dating, harassment, scamming, and sexuality (some of which were prefaced with a "read at your own risk" statement emphasizing the mature nature of the content) suggests that tweens' perspectives are being taken seriously. Instead of filtering all articles of controversial content, the editor uses the "editor's notes" section to support tweens in making appropriate decisions and to encourage their thinking about particular topics by raising questions.

At the same time, community management serves a role in giving different tools to players. For instance, players can choose to "silence" an offensive player and no longer hear what that player chats or whispers. Furthermore, players can report inappropriate behaviors to Whyville's 911 and the company will take various actions. Depending on the severity, punishments are imposed on the offending players, ranging from banning chat for a few days, visibly indicated by Band-Aids slapped onto avatars' mouths, to revoking one's account and thus forfeiting all face parts, salary, and clams. On any given day in Whyville, one can see avatars cruising public places wearing their Band-Aids like badges of honor. Also, losing one account does not prohibit players from using another one or opening a new one. More importantly, the articles in the *Whyville Times* provide a public forum for players themselves to discuss the appropriateness of offenses, thus establishing community norms. For instance, cheating and scamming are largely considered normal parts of game play that actively contribute to the vibrancy of the community.[18] On the other hand, behavior connected to overtly sexual flirting and dating and/or player safety is not considered a normal part of game play, and serious efforts are made to protect players from these behaviors.

Overall, the combination of chat filters, monitoring by city workers, youth-initiated behavior controls, and consequences for problematic behavior works to maintain a particular community standard for behavior while also giving tweens more freedom to chat and experiment than they might have in other virtual worlds that target younger players. The limited chat filter and the player-driven management tools are especially key in this regard because they allow players to tailor their experience in Whyville largely to their own perceived readiness to engage with topics related to sexuality, racial/ethnic identity, and so on.[19] They also provide a relatively safe space in which Whyvillians may practice how to appropriately respond in social situations that may be new to them (e.g., being "hit on" or asked out on a date) precisely because of the community management measures that are in place.[20]

Despite increasing trends of hundreds of millions of children playing in virtual settings,[21] it is unclear how community management measures provide enough openness to support responsible play, especially for children and youth. If, as Jenkins has argued, spaces for peer play are being constrained by discourses of safety and protection year after year,[22] how can we sponsor open areas where children can be imaginative in their play and learn to act responsibly? With earlier major developments in communicative technology (the telegraph, the telephone) moral panic has often ensued as adults worry about children's safety and moral character because of the influences of new technology.[23] However, we must be careful not to make the issues solely about protection and avoidance, which belittle children's agency and design. Instead, virtual worlds need to provide opportunities for responsible play with room for the development of innovative social practices and design among peers to sponsor learning and innovation.

Creative Play

We found creative play taking place in the open-ended spaces in the virtual world of Whyville, where tweens had more power over design, personal expression, and sharing with each other. Some of this creative play was designed for the players—especially the opportunity to create, sell, shop for, and assemble avatar parts. In contrast, other creative play was led by the players themselves—for instance in the relatively open space of chatting, where many tweens flirted, developed new forms of language that facilitated their needs and desires, and even worked creatively around chat filters. Creative play also took place beyond the site of Whyville, on cheat sites where players collaborated, shared knowledge, and invented ways to beat games not anticipated by the designers. These three areas highlight some of the intended (avatar design) and unintended (flirting, cheating) ways children play creatively in virtual worlds—a creativity that lends itself to constructionist learning, or learning by making in a social environment.

With hundreds of millions of participants, virtual worlds for children and youth are still untapped and understudied for their educational potential. Grimes argued that these worlds—left vacant by game designers and educators—have been largely created and driven by commercial companies that use them for product placement and advertising, acculturating children to consumerist practices and constraining their personal expression in their social play spaces.[24] Given that children's peer play is a significant place to look for innovation and creativity and that this innovation and creativity is essential for much productive learning, we must consider how to make virtual worlds spaces that allow enough freedom for creative expression.

If we think about the design opportunities in digital publics, we must surely allocate a prominent place to identity play in avatar designs. The complex design landscape of avatars in Whyville is vastly different from the limited menu of choices available for customizing one's appearance in many commercial virtual worlds.[25] In Whyville, the provision of all avatar content and interactions resides in the hands of players. Thus, the purposes for creating avatars differ from other games; the primary purpose is to enhance socialization between players, an important activity among tweens. Quite interestingly, this incredible range of customization has led to a number of hotly debated social issues in regard to avatars, including class stratification (newbie versus oldie), pressure to fit in with the latest trend, and even inequitable racial representation.

In Whyville we witnessed design changes over the years that responded to players' own comments and suggestions, for instance changing the standard peach potato-shaped smiley faces that were assigned to every newcomer to more customized appearances that allowed choices of several different skin colors and outfits. Even though newcomers are still easily identifiable because such sophisticated knowledge is required for using face parts in sync with Whyville's changing cultural norms of attractiveness, these changes have influenced how new players enter the space. From the very beginning everyone has an opportunity to decide on some aspects of personal representation, with the opportunity for more design freedom as income and skills grow. The top-down design changes based on players' bottom-up feedback illustrate that it is possible to change features in virtual worlds to take account for more diversity in avatar representation from the start. More importantly, it illustrates how digital publics can support more fluid notions of virtual identity, allowing for personal expression from the beginning and supporting small changes and experimentation with various looks (and even race and gender). It is important for tweens and others to play with representations of their "real" self or of a fantasy character, use various affinities to build different friendships, and even have the opportunity to use appearance for social activism.

As evidenced in the debates about avatar designs, participation in design promotes opportunities to become aware of playing in a designed world.

After all, if one realizes one is playing in a designed world, then one might realize that design can be changed. Engaging children in understanding and challenging the built-in assumptions of games and virtual worlds may encourage them not simply to reproduce commercial media or negative social practices (e.g., making fun of newbies) but to actively engage in creative design that disrupts such discourses.[26] The costume contest was an example of our own intervention that capitalized on an area of creative design to help children reflect on the social pressures to look a certain way in Whyville. As a result of the contest, we saw how avatar designs provided alternative creations that went against the local social norms and promoted tweens' thinking about how they treated others. Avatars provide a relatively easy opportunity to step into someone else's shoes by looking a certain way and seeing how others react. We need to seek out other opportunities that can promote children's reflections on the norms, values, and designs of games and virtual worlds. Creating playful interventions that capitalize on the creative affordances of virtual sites is one way to do so.

It is probably not a coincidence that two of the areas we highlighted as sites of creative play in Whyville involved push-backs against the intended design of the virtual world. In their flirting and development of cheats and cheat sites, Whyvillians went beyond the design of their virtual world and even the space of the virtual world itself to work around the social and technical limitations of Whyville. Significant opportunities for learning academically related skills are present in the designs of cheats and cheat sites in particular: technical skills from scripting to databases to Web hosting; media skills in building a following and earning money through advertisement; science skills involving the use and creation of representations and explanations; and creative skills in working around the technical designs of games, chat filters, and official social practices. As such, these transgressive designs provide a fertile learning context for leveraging virtual worlds more explicitly for children's design purposes.[27]

Conclusions

When play (or any other activity, for that matter) moves into the digital realm, we often assume differences from everyday life because on the surface it looks and feels different, at least to us adults. Indeed, what we observed and experienced in Whyville often felt like visiting foreign territory. When we first joined Whyville we were strangers entering a new culture—we didn't know dress protocols or how to speak the lingo, though we learned. Many speak of "digital natives"[28] when they see how current generations of kids and youth interact with and participate in new technologies, comparing them to adults who are digital "immigrants" who have encountered digital media relatively late in life. This impression is fueled by the apparent fearlessness and seeming ease with which kids approach digital technologies and virtual worlds. But is fearlessness and ease what we saw? Our observations suggest otherwise. The tweens we studied had to learn. When they first entered Whyville, it was unfamiliar territory, but they quickly adapted to the language conventions, navigation, and social protocols, often supported by friends they knew. It appears that the differences between online and offline play are more constructed in our minds, especially those of adults, than reflected in what we observed in tweens creating online representations, socializing with others, and engaging in boundary play. The challenges faced by kids in joining online play communities are not so different from what they face elsewhere.

Reimagining play in the digital public is not so much about envisioning an alternate reality as it is about understanding how play connects across multiple dimensions in designed worlds, and understanding how to provide adequate room for learning to play creatively and responsibly within, between, and outside of the boundaries of those worlds. This boundary play furnishes agency to players, not without challenges or dilemmas, but oftentimes empowering in ways that engage players' creativity. The examples of creative play point toward further affordances of virtual environments to offer a social forum for relationships that can develop around shared designs and other creative productions.

At the outset of this book, we argued that play in digital publics has the potential to provide participants with new forms to engage with and to creatively design for others, with implications for social development, creative expression, and learning. Supporting players in making connections to each other, to family and friends, to important values of respect and responsibility, and to their own creative agency is an important way to help play in digital publics live up to its potential. Fostering connectivity is where the future of play in the digital public will and should be.

Research Notes

We are obviously not the first researchers to study virtual worlds, but in 2002 when our research of Whyville.net started, engaging in virtual ethnography and surveying massive online communities were still relatively new approaches.[1] There was little consensus and collective experience on how to conduct research and how to participate as researchers in these worlds.[2] A strong divide also existed between the quantitative and qualitative methodologies to understand what, when, and why players engage in these communities.[3] Researchers addressed the challenges of studying virtual worlds by either collecting logfiles and large-scale surveys[4] or conducting in-depth observations and interviews, alongside participation in virtual and local spaces by the researchers themselves.[5] As we describe later in more detail, we happily crossed these dividing lines by collecting simultaneously quantitative and qualitative data and using multiple mixed methods[6] to address the challenges in researching the complexity of virtual worlds. Along the way, we also created new methodological approaches that further contribute to this burgeoning field of understanding the digital public.

The findings reported in this book are based on four consecutive studies that took place between 2002 and 2009. The first, exploratory study took place in 2002 when sixth grade teacher Cathleen Galas and her class of students joined Whyville and participated in WhyPox, the virtual epidemic, as part of their science curriculum. We returned in 2004–2005 and set up a more comprehensive study that not only examined but also designed Whyville interventions together with Galas and implemented them in her classrooms. In addition we set up an after-school club during 2005 that included extensive observations and analyses of online play and collected logfile data and surveys from nearly 600 participants.[7] Two later studies were more focused in nature; one in early 2008 took place again in an after-school club and examined avatar design and play, while the other in late 2009 surveyed Whyville members about their online flirting and dating. In several instances, there was a significant time lag between data collection (2005) and analyses that stretched well into 2009, owing to the size and complexity of the data set. Thus, member-checking with online or offline participants was no longer an option for us. The research included in this book draws on different sets of data sources, mostly in an effort to compensate for this shortcoming and to allow us to triangulate our findings. We report here in more detail on our methods and the choices we made to counterbalance the more casual tone of our writings here, which we've adopted to make our findings accessible to a larger audience.

Recruiting Study Participants

In late 2004, we began to recruit online participants via announcements and in public online sessions on the Whyville website (see also Acknowledgments). We asked them to sign parental consent and assent forms in which they agreed to participate in the research study, and most importantly, allowed us to track their movements and interactions online. Over the following weeks, close to 600 of those consent forms came back to us, some via email, many via fax, and hundreds via mail. We did check out a few where signatures looked suspicious by calling the participants. The online sample that we recruited for this study was representative of Whyville's demographics: like Whyville's general population, our recruits were mostly at the middle-school level, ranging between ten and fourteen years old (12.3 years median), and 68 percent of our participants were female. So, whenever we refer to logfile results, they come from this pool of online participants.

We also recruited participants from the after-school club, where about twenty tweens ages nine to twelve years (fourth through sixth grade) visited for an hour most days after school from January to March 2005. Enrollment and visits to the club were voluntary, and members were free to spend time in Whyville on whatever they wanted to do. In addition, six members of the after-school club were sixth graders (eleven to twelve years old) who also played on Whyville during science class as part of a unit on studying viruses and epidemics.[8] The teacher had agreed to integrate Whyville activities into her science curriculum on infectious diseases.

In early 2008, we again set up an after-school club in the same school, this time with eight students between the ages of ten and twelve years, four boys and four girls, who came for a period of eight weeks to play on Whyville. In later 2009, together with researchers from the University of Southern California, we collected online surveys on 630 Whyville members' flirting and dating behavior, but there was no offline data collection from kids in clubs or classes.

Collecting Data

In our data collection, we included online surveys that focused on different aspects of Whyville life and Whyvillians' interests in technology and science. The students in science classes and members of the club took those surveys as well. The 2005 surveys (split into three parts) were administered online, and each participant received clams for completing them. The surveys contained mostly multiple-choice items and some open-ended questions asking about players' interest and attitudes in technology and science, their understanding of and experiences with WhyPox, and general assessments about their preferences for a range of Whyville activities such as avatar design, importance of salary and clams, and interaction with others. The 2009 survey on online socializing was more focused and included questions about the importance of online relationships, parents' knowledge about such relationships, sources for finding information about relationships, and dating. More detail on these findings can be found in several publications.[9]

In addition, we observed online play on a daily basis, especially during the three months of the Whypox outbreak. Other Whyville resources, such as the *Whyville Times*, were also consulted for what Whyvillians wrote about different topics. The online newspaper archive contains over 10,000 searchable and publicly available articles that citizens of Whyville have written about nearly every conceivable topic. For more specific analyses on cheating, flirting, avatar design, and WhyPox, we searched with related keywords for pertinent articles. As noted, Whyvillians also maintain websites outside of Whyville to showcase their insider knowledge of Whyville customs and cheats on games. Hundreds of these sites are available just be typing "cheat" and "Whyville" into any search engine.

We received tracking data from Numedeon of 595 online and after-school players that gave us comprehensive logfiles of every click and chat exchange by consenting Whyvillians.[10] Numedeon, the owner and creator company of Whyville, gathered click-level and chat data on each participant between January and June 2005. This means that every time a participant clicked to go to a new space on Whyville, this was recorded, in addition to every word they typed in chat or the whisper bubbles in chat spaces. This large set of data contained over 9 million data points, which we used later for establishing player profiles and case studies.

We also conducted observations of twenty kids in the after-school club in winter 2005 to get a sense of how the social setting and interactions structured play and participation in Whyville both online and offline. In the after-school club, ten computers in two rooms were accessible to players, who often ended up sharing a computer or wandering around the room talking to others.[11] In addition, forty-seven students from the two science classes participated in Whyville; however, their choices during the class were more directed than the open-ended play in the club. But we could not ignore relationships among class members as a social context of learning in Whyville, as became apparent in our findings. The observations were captured in field notes that supplemented recordings of two video cameras moving between computer stations recording small group interactions between January and March 2005 in both the club and the class. In addition, we conducted debriefing interviews with most club participants and about one-third of the class participants, following an open-ended interview guideline that asked each member about favorite activities, why and how often they changed their looks, and how they learned in Whyville. These interviews lasted between fifteen and twenty minutes each. Our process of documenting activities with field notes, video recordings, and debriefing interviews was much the same in our 2008 study of the after-school club, with the distinction that three researchers wrote field notes and we focused additional effort on studying participants' avatar designs, collecting screenshots of their avatars everyday of the club. In the middle of the study, we gave each participant one hundred clams and asked them to create avatars of their choosing as part of a costume contest intervention.

Analyzing Data

We approached the analyses of data with a particular issue in mind, such as understanding engagement and participation in the virtual epidemic or discussions about race and looks in avatar design, but often we combined multiple data sources to triangulate our findings. For instance, in studying avatar design, we included not only logfiles to understand the frequency and thus relevance of avatar-related activities among players, but also articles written in the *Whyville Times* about this very topic as well as analyses of talk online and in the after-school clubs; sometimes, we even mined chat content for certain word frequencies.

More importantly, we connected the quantitative and qualitative analyses of logfile data for profiles of players and case studies of players or practices. We first developed player profiles by using logfiles consisting of over 9 million data points indicating location visits and activities over a six-month time period (approximately twenty-six weeks). In order to analyze individual patterns of participation within Whyville, we created thirteen categories of locations and activities: (1) ymail: email, (2) whypox: Whypox related activities, (3) whisper: private chatting, (4) social: social activities, (5) multigame: multiplayer gaming, (6) misc: miscellaneous activities, (7) info-com: information seeking, (8) house: house-construction games, (9) games: games for salary, (10) face: avatar related activities, (11) economic: economic activities, (12) chat, and (13) bbs: bulletin-board reading or posting. Because player participation in each of these categories ranged from 0 to 92,407 visits or clicks over six months, raw and standardized number (mean = 0 and SD = 1) of visits were used in various analyses to simplify interpretation. Raw numbers were used to describe player participation among the thirteen categories. To create and identify player profiles, or groups of similar players, we used standardized numbers in a two-step cluster analysis.[12] Positive standardized values indicate greater than average (50th percentile) participation, while negative values indicate less than average (50th percentile) participation.

In addition to these aggregated analyses, we decided to approach the logfile data with two other perspectives in the relatively new tradition of connective ethnography in studying people across spaces and times.[13] In one, the *person* perspective, we wanted to build case studies of players that recreated their participation over time, while in the other, the *practice* perspective, we wanted to develop an account of how a particular gaming practice was adopted over time. In both cases, we used logfile data to capture the "who, when, how, and where" but supplemented this with information available from field notes, video records, and interviews. Making sense of logfiles qualitatively, especially longitudinally following one person or one practice over several months, is challenging and unusual, and it represents one of the methodological contributions of our work.[14]

We used the findings from these player profiles to construct qualitative case studies of individual players.[15] For instance, in choosing Zoe/bluwave, one of the club members, we selected someone who we knew had a fairly high participation rate in Whyville based on her placement in the profile analysis described above as well as her interactions in the club. We first created minute-by-minute summaries by isolating her logfiles and going click by click through the data. Then we condensed these into short daily narratives that noted patterns and innovations in participation. Each line of her logfiles contained her username, a time stamp, her location in Whyville, and, if applicable, chat or whisper text. In all there were over 54,000 lines of text in bluwave's logfiles. To create the minute-by-minute summaries, we sampled the days she was on Whyville, selecting the first seven days and then alternating every five or six days to ensure breadth of days of the week in our sample. In all, we analyzed thirty-five days during her first two months on Whyville from January to June 2005. In our final interpretation of Zoe/bluwave's activities, we also took into account video, field notes, and interview data from the club while looking for consensus or discrepancies between her activities and "ways of being."

We used similar techniques for tracing particular practices, such as teleporting, giving a secret command, or throwing projectiles such as mudballs, a popular practice in Whyville among club members. Once we identified teleporting as a practice to study (a process that involved significant immersion in the data), we conducted three kinds of analyses. First, we searched the logfiles for the first time that club members teleported and identified their physical locations based on time stamps and knowledge of attendance and schedules at the club and in the classrooms. Second, using these time stamps as starting points, we pieced together information across all of our data (logfiles, field notes, videos, and interviews) to determine the process and contexts in which each club member learned to teleport. Inevitably there was more information about some individuals than others, but in every case we determined social, spatial contexts of knowledge sharing and diffusion. Finally, we inductively and thematically coded incidents of peer-to-peer teaching of teleporting across the data. For the logfiles, this involved identifying times when teleporting was discussed rather than used for transportation (e.g., "how do u teleport" versus "teleport moon") and assembling conversations in the logfiles between school members before coding them. We used a similar approach for projectile throwing, identifying times, spaces, and social contexts of learning and tracing key events backward and forward in the data to establish histories that led up to and followed learning how to throw projectiles.

Limitations

With all these data and different analyses, our interpretations are by no means an exhaustive account of what happened in Whyville, online or offline, during this time. We received logfiles linked to player names, but the chat files often only gave us one side of the conversation since only consenting players' data were included in our data set. Like listening to a phone conversation, we thus were left to guess at what others were saying. An exception was with club and class members whose conversations we could follow online by focusing on a single time and space and eliminating other players in order to reconstruct online conversations, sometimes synchronizing this with talk in the club caught on video or in field notes. We also chose not collect some information such as the content of email (ymail) that we considered private, although we do know that ymailing was a frequent activity Whyvillians engaged in, in particular to follow up encounters. We also only recorded screen shots of what their avatars looked like and some on-screen movements in the 2008 club. It is clearly impossible to capture everything that is going on in the many spaces of a virtual world. And even if one were to capture everything, the challenge of making sense of it remains.[16]

Chapter Notes

1 Playgrounds for Millions

1. Zoe and her username "bluwave," as well as all other names of all kids or Whyville players throughout the book, are pseudonyms, with the exception of the names of authors of *Whyville Times* articles that are public. In chapter 2, we will present a more detailed study of Zoe's life in Whyville; see also Fields and Kafai 2012. In this book we call our virtual world players either "kids" or "tweens" because they fall into the age range of nine to twelve years, which makes them not quite adolescents but no longer children.

2. Research on virtual worlds for kids, unlike those of adults, is rare, with the exception of work by Jackie Marsh (2008), Mitzuko Ito (2010), and Rebecca Black (2010).

3. The term "digital publics" is based on danah boyd's (2007) definition of networked publics as consisting of a mediated space that provides "teens with a space to work out identity and status, make sense of cultural cues, and negotiate public life" (p. 121). In her research, boyd focuses on social networking sites such as MySpace or Facebook, where participants, represented by themselves, are socializing with others. By contrast, virtual worlds, whose players are represented by avatars, can (but do not always) provide opportunities to generate content other than messages in addition to social networking among participants. The boundaries between social networking sites and virtual worlds are constantly being redrawn, as many social networking sites now also offer games as well, for instance Facebook's Farmville. We use "digital publics" as an umbrella term to encompass the many spaces that are part of virtual worlds.

4. Jenkins (1998/2005) first made the argument that video games provided new spaces for play since adults had started limiting unsupervised play in neighborhoods and malls.

5. While we hear often how many millions play in adult gaming sites such as World of Warcraft (18 million), or participated in the now defunct virtual worlds of Teen Second Life (21 million), virtual worlds for kids significantly surpass these

numbers. For instance, Habbo Hotel has 230 million, followed by Poptropica with 75 million, and Neopets with 54 million registered players. Many commercial virtual worlds don't publish their numbers because they consider this information proprietary.

6. Grimes and Fields (2012) coined the term "networking residue" to describe the traces of online interactions that are captured and can be distributed further by others.

7. According to danah boyd (2007), participation in the networked publics, and by extension play in virtual worlds, is defined by persistence of actions and interactions that become recorded, searchable, and replicable to invisible audiences.

8. Several researchers have written extensively about how designers often carry their own assumptions into designs replicating stereotypes and constraining design choices (Taylor 2006) and how values become embedded in the designs of games (Flanagan and Nussbaum 2008).

9. For more extensive treatments on the role of children's play across cultures, age, gender, spaces, and media, see the work by Doris Fromberg and Doris Bergen (2006), Marjorie Harness Goodwin (2006), Iona Opie and Peter Opie (1969), and Jerome Singer and Dorothy Singer (1992, 2005), to name just a few.

10. Lev Vygotsky (1933/1978) already pointed to pretend play as a formative area of development where children process the rules and roles of the culture around them as they playact scenarios that mirror real-life cultural rules. Among preadolescent peer cultures, children work through their desires for sharing and social culture as well as control over their lives through interaction with peers (Corsaro 2005). To achieve these desires, children create alliances and rally an audience in their play by demonstrating an understanding of a game through producing variations of the game (Garvey 1984), keying characteristic voices and speaking styles (Kyratzis 2004), and excluding others through talk (Goodwin 2002).

11. See Piaget's (1951) work on play, dreams, and imitation.

12. Here we reference work by Marina Bers (2011) that focuses on building interpersonal skills in competence, confidence, and character as well as intrapersonal skills in caring, connection, and community in the context of the positive technological development framework. The research by Henry Jenkins and colleagues (2006) focuses on participatory challenges and examines critical skills involving participation and production skills, ethical challenges, and transparency issues in the context of media literacy. Researchers from the learning technology side often focus on technology fluency skills, highlighting various technical skills such as understanding systems and devices (see NRC 2000).

13. See Goodwin 1985.

14. Ibid., 315.

15. For recent examples of ethnographies of adult gaming communities and virtual worlds, see Boellstorff 2008, Castronova 2006, Pearce 2011, Steinkuehler 2006, and Taylor 2006.

16. See the report by Jenkins and colleagues (2006) on confronting the challenges of participatory culture.

17. See Ito et al. 2010.

18. See report by James and colleagues (2009) on youth ethics in participatory culture (more on this also in chapter 5).

19. See the article on safeguarding play by Kafai and Searle (2011).

20. In his keynote at the 2012 Games, Learning and Society conference in Madison, Wisconsin, Sebastian Deterding referred to "deviant playfulness." See also Deterding et al. 2011.

21. The demographic information about Whyville's player population can be found on the website as reported by Numedeon, Inc. At the time when we conducted our research, the player population was similar in demographics but counted only 1.2 million registered players.

22. The demographic information about Habbo Hotel was provided by "Habbo Hotel—Check In to Check It Out!," http://www.sulake.com/habbo/.

23. These numbers come from Solis (2010). Demographic information about Neopets was retrieved from http://www.quantcast.com/neopets.com.

24. The term "sticky" refers to a website's ability to keep visitors on the site once they have navigated there or encourage them to return to the site frequently. See http://www.webopedia.com/TERM/S/sticky.html.

25. One thread of studies has focused largely on online play, most prevalently perhaps the first-person accounts in which researchers use their own learning experiences and reflections in conjunction with ethnographic studies (e.g., Boellstorff 2008; Castronova 2006; Steinkuehler 2006; Taylor 2006) to document various social, economic, and cultural practices in youth and adult gaming sites and virtual worlds. Others have launched large-scale surveys inviting thousands of youth and adult players to respond to various aspects of their gaming experiences (Williams, Yee, and Caplan 2008; Yee 2008). A few studies have used tracking data to capture players' movements across multiple spaces and time zones; Ducheneaut, Yee, Nickell, and Moore (2006) studied guild and social networks in the online game World of Warcraft, and Nardi, Ly, and Harris (2007) analyzed chat to understand how players learned from each other in spontaneous, contextual conversations "driven by small events."

26. Several other researchers have noted the particular research issues and ethics of conducting research online (see Kraut, Olson, Banaji, Bruckman, Cohen, and Couper,

2004). We discuss some aspects of our research methods in chapter 2 and in more detail in Research Notes, a special section at the end of the book.

27. In Internet culture, a lurker is a person who reads discussions on a message board, newsgroup, chatroom, file sharing site, social networking site, or listens to people in VOIP calls such as Skype and Ventrilo or other interactive systems, but rarely or never participates actively. See http://en.wikipedia.org/wiki/Lurking.

28. See the Research Notes for more detail on our methods for tracking user data in log files.

29. See Kafai and Searle 2012. However, discovery of these instances of illicit or inappropriate behavior occurred two to three years after the activities occurred because analysis took a long time, so we did not contact kids or parents about these activities. When we did observe problematic behavior in person during the after-school club or class, teachers at the school discussed boundaries and ethics with the participants.

2   Digital Footprints

1. EIEmAyeOh 2011.

2. See, e.g., the 2010 Pew Internet and American Life Project (Lenhart, Purcell, Smith, and Zickuhr 2010). For exceptions, see the 2011 EU Kids Online study, which include kids as young as nine (Livingstone, Haddon, Gorzig, and Olafsson 2011) or the 2010 Kaiser Family Foundation study, which includes kids as young as eight (Rideout, Foehr, and Roberts 2010). One exception to this trend is a recent study commissioned by Common Sense Media (2011) that focused solely on children from birth through eight years old and their media use, including computers and video games.

3. For a review of recent literature on what we know about kids' social practices online, see Grimes and Fields 2012.

4. For the importance of strong and weak ties, see the work by Granovetter (1973) that examined community relationships. This concept of strong and weak ties has also now been applied to online relationships. A related study by Steinfield, Ellison, and Lampe (2008) showed that using Facebook more intensely especially helped teens who had lower self-esteem. Teens were able to follow acquaintances at school whom they knew but with whom they were not especially close.

5. Parts of this section reprinted with the permission of Cambridge University Press from Fields and Kafai 2012.

6. We created the pseudonym "bluwave" to mirror the shining of her original username. The theme of angels and shining came up as Zoe described in an interview in March 2005 her avatar sometimes appearing as an angel with wings (halos and wings are commonly available on Whyville).

7. To protect club members' privacy, we never mention participants by name. All names and usernames are made up, though we attempt to reflect some of their personality in the names we chose for them.

8. For a detailed account of teleporting and knowledge diffusion, see Fields and Kafai 2009, parts of which are reprinted here with kind permission from Springer Science+Business Media.

9. The only exception to this would be learning from an online written record of insider knowledge, namely, an exceptional cheat site where they might be listed among other "newbie" hints (Fields and Kafai 2010b). Based on analysis of the data where we specifically looked for how and whether members used cheats, we are very confident that club members did not learn about teleporting from cheat sites, so it must have been learned from others more directly.

10. Also, because teleporting is accomplished by typing a specific command, "teleport moon" (or "teleport [place]"), each teleport action is visible in the chat records that are part of the logfiles we collected. We could easily search for the occasions when the word "teleport" was typed and each time find that a participant had been teleported.

11. See Hutchins 1995.

12. Ching and Kafai 2008.

13. James Gee encapsulates this kind of cultural learning as big-D Discourse: "ways of thinking, acting, interacting, valuing, feeling, believing, and using symbols, tools, and objects in the right places and at the right times" (Gee 1999, 13). Constance Steinkuehler (2006) describes a similar episode of her learning the discourse of an online gaming community through hunting practices.

14. With help from Dr. David Feldon and Dr. Michael Giang, we performed a few different analyses on the kids' clicks and chats to unpack their behavior.

15. See Feldon and Kafai 2008.

16. Giang, Kafai, Fields, and Searle 2012.

17. See Research Notes for details on cluster analyses.

18. Several other studies of mostly adult multiplayer online communities have confirmed this finding using logfile analyses (Williams, Yee, and Caplan 2008) and surveys (Yee 2006).

19. Prensky 2001.

20. Hargittai and Walejko 2008.

21. Ito, Horst, Bittanti, and Boyd 2010.

3   Identity Play

1. Tami324 2000.

2. Akbar's, the online face parts mall in Whyville, offers the option for face-part buyers to shop by category. We used this embedded category structure to organize our search for heads and bodies in different colors. In September 2006, Akbar's offered 137 blank heads designed to serve as a backdrop for putting together your own unique Whyville face and 743 bodies (torsos complete with clothing) to complete the look. All these parts were created by Whyvillians. Looking only at skin colors that were available naturally (i.e., we did not count or study fantasy skin colors such as blue, white, or bright orange), we divided available blank heads into four color categories. To confirm that our visual judgments of peach, brown, olive, and yellow colors did not have overlapping boundaries or inconsistencies, we used Adobe Photoshop to assess the red, green, blue (RGB) value for each shade of head and checked that the numerical parameters for what we had labeled peach, brown, olive, and yellow face parts did not overlap. We then captured screenshots of all the non-peach heads and bodies and collected information on the name and manufacturer of each face part. Reprinted with permission from Sage Publications from Kafai, Cook, and Fields 2010.

3. For more detail, see the description of why kids made their avatars the way they did in Kafai, Fields, and Cook 2010.

4. Kolko 1998, 240.

5. Turkle 1984.

6. Turkle 1995.

7. For examples, see Berman and Bruckman 2001 and Taylor 1999.

8. Erikson (1968) popularized the idea that coming to a concrete understanding of self (identity) was a key accomplishment of adolescence in Western culture. From this perspective, individuals question, judge, self-reflect, experiment, and eventually commit to a core idea about themselves in relation to the core of their culture. An alternative view sees identity not as a core sense of self but as a set of "long-term, living relations between persons and their place and participation in communities of practice" (Lave and Wenger 1991, 53). This sense of the word frames identity as a process of social activity enacted in practice. We interpret identity both as how a person thinks about him- or herself as well as how a person acts in practice (Fields and Enyedy 2013). Thus, throughout this book we emphasize both what kids do in Whyville and the meanings they make of their own actions.

9. Larson 2000; Lloyd and Duveen 1992.

10. Two studies of online teen chatrooms that analyzed 12,000 utterances from 1,100 participants found that identity presentation (Subrahmanyam, Šmahel, and

Greenfield 2006), partner selection (Šmahel and Subrahmanyam 2007), and sexual comments (Subrahmanyam et al. 2006) were the most frequent kinds of utterances in chatrooms. This is unsurprising given that teens are exploring romantic relationships, close friendships, and "who they are" in their everyday lives as well.

11. Kroger 2000; Phinney 1989.

12. Tynes, García, Giang, and Coleman (2010) analyzed the discourses of 48 groups on Facebook and MySpace dedicated to issues of race and ethnicity and found that kids talked about "advocacy, education, heritage and identity exploration, creation of racial safe havens, and general discussions of race" (21). Kids negotiated who they were in social discourse with each other, deciding who counted as Asian or black, sharing some of their challenges related to their looks or other aspects of their ethnicity (languages, dispersed relatives, which communities they felt accepted them), and even signing petitions that allowed them to take social action. Notably they claim that this was just as important for white youth as for others.

13. For more on a sociocultural perspective on identity see Fields and Enyedy 2013; Gee 2000–2001; Holland, Lachicotte, Skinner, and Cain 1998; Lave and Wenger 1991.

14. See Feldon and Kafai 2008 and Yee 2006.

15. Boellstorff 2008.

16. Lee and Hoadley 2007.

17. The only exceptions are the animated face parts that are created by Numedeon (about thirty parts in all).

18. For more, see Boellstorff's (2008) analysis of Second Life design tools as well as Kafai, Fields, and Cook's (2010) analysis of Whyville design tools.

19. Lucetta described her background as having twenty-seven different aspects and did not like to categorize herself as any one ethnic category (certainly not "mixed race").

20. Nakamura (2001) and others have argued that the Internet and games, like all other media, mirror the racial stereotyping found in society. Comparisons of monitored and unmonitored chatrooms found that teens weave racial references, slurs, and identifiers in their online conversations (Tynes, Reynolds, and Greenfield, 2004).

21. Leander and Frank (2006) use the metaphor of lamination to explain the identity work in youths' remixing of digital media and how these new assemblages help the youth position themselves in social online affinity spaces. They emphasize that, in laminates, "one can continue to find the traces of social, cultural, and personal resources, and continue to recognize tensions and contradictions among these resources" (187). At the same time, through the compression of multiple layers (a

characteristic of how something becomes a laminate), laminated artifacts take on properties distinct from their constitutive elements. Further, different aspects of these artifacts can be highlighted by different communities, facilitating the foregrounding of certain identities with some people and other identities with others. Thus, both the process of making these digitally layered objects and the objects themselves draw together personal (psychological), social, and cultural elements to make something unique.

22. "Expressing Yourself through Face Parts" (2002).

23. Sweden 2005.

4   Social Play

1. XKaileeX 2003.

2. Aquagerl 2002.

3. In her book *Alone Together*, Sherry Turkle (2011) argues persuasively that computers are becoming the architecture for our social lives. Whether or not you believe this to be true, it is certainly interesting to consider the ways that computers and various software mediate and shape interactions between people.

4. See the 2009 Kaiser Family Foundation Reports (Rideout, Foehr, and Roberts 2010).

5. See Ito et al. 2010.

6. See Subrahmanyam, Greenfield, and Tynes 2004 for a study of young adults' chatroom behavior. Further, Subrahmanyam, Reich, Waechter, and Espinoza (2008) suggest that kids (in this case teens) use virtual environments like social networking sites to pursue a developmental agenda to find romantic partners.

7. Elkind 1979.

8. Cook and Kaiser 2004.

9. Granovetter 1973.

10. See Ellison, Steinfield, and Lampe 2007; Subrahmanyam, Reich, Waechter, and Espinoza 2008; Lenhart and Madden 2007.

11. A study by Ünlüsoy and de Haan 2011 in the Netherlands found that youth with non-Dutch backgrounds (Moroccan-Dutch, Turkish-Dutch, and others) had social networks that were more globally distributed than Dutch-only youth.

12. Other studies of immigrant (especially second-generation) youth have documented the ways that their online social networking can help them keep up (or learn) multiple languages important to their hybrid ethnic heritages (e.g., Lam 2000;

2009), build transnational identities and spaces to consider the hybridity of their cultures (Skop and Adams 2009), and discuss topics unique to their personal histories (Lee and Hoadley 2006). Though these studies do not apply specifically to virtual worlds, there are similarities between the social networking opportunities in virtual worlds and other online social networking activities such as instant messaging (IM), social network sites, and other forums (Grimes and Fields 2012). Leander, Phillips, and Taylor (2010) provide an excellent review of this literature, as well as of other considerations of virtual geographies of kids' relationships as they build and extend social spaces online.

13. Steinfield, Ellison, and Lampe 2008.

14. See Tynes 2007a,b.

15. Parts of this section are drawn from Fields and Kafai 2010a.

16. For more details on projectile throwing, see Fields and Kafai 2010a. Projectile throwing on Whyville involved purchasing any number of different throwable materials: from the generic faces (smiley, sad, winking) and sports paraphernalia (Frisbees, footballs, baseballs) to gross materials (mudballs, maggots, garlic) and cute objects (puckered lips, hearts, rainbows). After purchasing these materials for one to six clams, one could aim at a person or a direction (i.e., degrees in a circle from 0 to 259) and "throw" the projectile. For example, Blake might type, "throw mudball bluwave." A mudball would appear next to Blake, travel in a straight line toward Zoe/bluwave, and, if no one was in the way, hit Zoe and stick to her for a few seconds before disappearing. As one might imagine, this became a highly engaging activity in the club with many variations, from mudball wars to flirting.

17. See Thorne 1993.

18. See Subrahmanyam, Greenfield, and Tynes 2004.

19. Parts of this section were drawn with permission from Giang, Kafai, Fields, and Searle 2012 and Kafai, Fields, and Searle 2010.

20. Elkind 1979.

21. Thorne 1993; Walkerdine 2007.

22. See Holiday50 2008.

23. Of the fifty-five articles we studied, published in the *Whyville Times* between 2002 and 2008, twelve articles had a definite pro-Whydating stance, more than double (thirty-three) articulated an anti-Whydating view, and six took a neutral stance or did not specifically address dating practices.

24. Liss22 and Piker 2002.

25. Mikay37 2003.

26. KamuiX 2002.

27. Holiday50 2008.

28. Ibid.

29. Lilly2000 2000.

30. Punkst3r 2000.

31. xXOscarXx 2003.

32. JasmineK 2004.

33. Casc302 2006.

34. In 2009, we advertised and conducted an online survey about flirting and dating in Whyville. Whyville users between eight and fourteen were randomly recruited for an anonymous online survey. All Whyville users logging into the system in January 2009 were prompted by a recruitment message with a link. Kids who showed initial interests were contacted with more detailed information including a link to assent forms for their parents and a complete list of the survey questions. Only participants who were between eight and fourteen and whose parents assented were recruited for the survey. The total number of survey responses was 3,052. Gender distribution of the respondents was 80 percent girls (n=2442) and 20 percent boys (n=610). On average, the number of daily visit to Whyville was 0.57 with a standard deviation of 0.31. The mean membership period of the respondents was 14.85 months.

35. In terms of what relationships consist of in Whyville, we found that whether or not they had virtual girlfriends or boyfriends, tweens overwhelmingly emphasized that having a boyfriend or girlfriend involved mostly lighthearted and playful activities. The most common perceived activities listed for boyfriends and girlfriends were (1) complimenting each other on looks (80.98 percent), (2) spending time in private spaces (71.74 percent), (3) buying gifts for each other (68.48 percent), (4) sending clams (57.61 percent), (5) making out (50 percent), (6) throwing projectiles (32.07 percent), (7) sharing passwords (20.11 percent). Since only 21 percent of respondents claimed to have a girlfriend or boyfriend in Whyville, many of these activities reported by the larger survey population may only be what they *perceive* boyfriends and girlfriends do in Whyville. Who do tweens go to in order to find information about dating and relationships? In our survey tweens prioritized friends they knew in person (76.9 percent of the same gender and 53 percent of the opposite gender) as well as parents (54.7 percent) and more rarely teachers (33.7 percent).

36. See Epstein and Ward 2008.

37. Common Sense Media (2011).

38. For instance, see the spikes recorded in projectile throwing (Fields and Kafai 2010a) and teleporting (Fields and Kafai 2009).

5   Boundary Play

1. RachelJay 2002.

2. Parts of this section reprinted with the permission of Cambridge University Press from Fields and Kafai 2012.

3. The way we created the three categories of players was through a cluster analysis of their clicks, so it would be more accurate to say that the number of clicks that Blake made on Whyville quintupled. Mostly this happened through his chat—each chat entry counts as one quantitative entry. Still, we also see through our qualitative analysis that during his first four months his time spent on Whyville ranged from 8 to 80 minutes day (when he logged in), but from mid-May to mid-June, his time spent jumped to 140–650 minutes, logging in nearly every day for a month. That's quite a leap in time spent.

4. See Consalvo 2007.

5. See Steinkuehler and Duncan 2009.

6. See MacCabe, Trevino, and Butterfield 2001. Not only students but also parents and school administrators might have differing views on cheating. A recent incident illustrated that when a high school teacher failed students because of plagiarized homework, the principal reinstated students' grades, bowing to pressure from the school board and parents (Wilgoren 2002). Some studies show significant differences between students', teachers', and parents' judgments and rationales about appropriate uses of computers and the Internet (Kafai, Nixon, and Burnam 2007).

7. In the report "Young People, Ethics, and the New Digital Media," Harvard researchers James, Davis, Flores, Francis, Pettingill, Rundle and Gardner (2009) present a synthesis from interviews and research that outline five areas—identity, privacy, ownership and authorship, credibility, and participation—that they consider critical in ethical play with digital media.

8. James et al. 2009, 80.

9. For a full description, see Salen and Zimmerman 2004.

10. For more details on this study, see Fields and Kafai 2010b. To study the range of cheat sites about Whyville, we first did an Internet search by Googling the terms "Whyville cheat or cheats" in July 2006, which resulted in a listing of 257 sites. We looked up the sites listed in the first four pages of the search—38 sites in all (or approximately 15 percent of the total sites returned in our search)—presuming that the first websites turned up in the search were the ones Whyvillians would also be more likely to visit. Because 23 of the sites were scams, we focused our analysis on the 13 legitimate cheat sites. First, we looked for the range of cheats across the sites, drawing on typology developed by Salen and Zimmerman (2004). Then, using grounded theory (Glaser and Strauss 1967), we thematically coded the different

kinds of sites and the range of cheats for the games that resulted in salary raises (the most predominant form of cheats). For the latter, we built on Aschbacher's (2003) analysis of the cognitive skills and scientific problem solving in most of the salary-raising science games. As a validation of our classification of cheat sites, we found one website that provided an evaluation (one to five stars) of cheat sites that matched our own.

Through this process, we discovered that two of the cheat sites were much more nuanced and provided many more cheats and insider tips about participating socially in Whyville than the other sites. We conducted a case study of one of these sites, the most popular and most in-depth cheat site, GameSite.net (a pseudonym). From July to December 2006, we visited the site weekly and took screen shots of the changing forum discussions and welcome page of the site. In particular, we closely followed discussions and the development of a new cheat that coincided with the appearance of a new salary-raising science game in Whyville. In this way, we were able to study some of the active work of designing and participating in cheat sites.

This endnote reprinted with permission from Sage Publications, Fields and Kafai 2010b.

11. Scam sites formed the majority of the websites listed as Whyville cheat sites (25 out of 36 sites we selected).

12. About a year after our study, this website came to a close as the lead designer/ owner decided to focus more on other technical hobbies like making videos.

13. See Consalvo 2007; Gee 2003.

14. Ickamcoy 2003.

15. GrriesYEA 2003.

16. Other writers have discussed the challenge of having multiple accounts on Whyville and whether in such cases votes should be counted by accounts or by the person behind the count. Several argued that multiple accounts used by the same individual should be allowed one vote each if the accounts represent active citizens on Whyville.

17. PixiBritt 2005.

18. Engeström 2008.

19. Norman 2005, 1. See also http://ubiquity.acm.org/article.cfm?id=1066347.

6   Science Play

1. Theboy2 2003.

2. See Bainbridge 2007.

3. Previous research studies have shown that many children have difficulties understanding how disease spreads and how to prevent disease from occurring (Au and Romo 1999; Kalish 1999; Obeidallah et al. 1993; Siegal 1988; Siegal and Peterson 1999; Sigelman, Estrada, Derenowski, and Woods 1996; Solomon and Cassimatis 1999). Most children learn about infectious diseases in school from textbooks by studying aspects such as the biology of germs (Au and Romo 1999) or historic outbreaks. Sometimes instructional activities also include participatory simulations that use hands-on classroom experiments or educational technologies to help students better understand aspects such as latency and immunity (Colella 2000) or the probability of getting a disease (Wilensky and Stroup 1999). We expected that allowing children to experience infectious disease virtually would make these historically difficult concepts for them more tangible and therefore more approachable.

4. The WhyPox epidemic is not the first instance of an epidemic in a virtual community. As early as in May 2000, BBC News reported that lethal guinea pigs had killed Sims players who had adopted them as virtual pets.

5. DiGsTeR02 2005.

6. See Lofgren and Fefferman 2007.

7. In these analyses of the simulator uses, we excluded the students because we already knew that they used the simulators as part of their science class activities. We wanted to know whether players would engage in scientific inquiry while gaming in their free time. More detail on how these analyses were performed can be found in Kafai, Quintero, and Feldon 2010.

8. Previous research has argued that people (especially children) typically approach scientific experimentation from one of two different perspectives (Kuhn and Phelps 1982; Schauble 1990; Shavelson, Baxter, and Gao 1993). Schauble, Klopfer, and Raghavan (1991) characterize experimentation approaches as representing either *engineering* goals or *scientific* goals. Those players with engineering goals attempt to create specific outcomes (e.g., the fastest, the biggest, or the most stable values for the dependent variables) without trying to validate general causal principles across contexts (i.e., simulation settings). While using the CDC simulators, the desired goal might be to have the greatest number of infections in the shortest amount of time or the fewest infections overall. In contrast, scientific goals entail an attempt to understand the causal relationships between the independent and dependent variables rather than to attain specific results (e.g., understanding how each controllable factor in the simulation affects the rate of infection or the total number of infections). Therefore, the outcomes of experiments conducted by individual players with scientific goals are typically found for a broad range of independent variable values instead of a narrow range that produces only specific, targeted outcomes. This dichotomy represents differences in fundamental approaches to scientific problem solving that characterize their understandings of what "doing science" means. Further, it draws an important distinction between players who attempt to test a

causal model to understand the mechanisms of disease and those whose first priority is to generate specific outcomes.

9. Lemke 1990, 1.

10. When analyzing the chat interactions before, during, and after the outbreak of WhyPox, we found that the frequency of these terms increased significantly during the WhyPox outbreak and then disappeared again. For more detail on this analysis of chat records, see Kafai, Quintero, and Feldon 2010.

11. Science education sees argumentation as central to the practice of science. Numerous studies have focused on the particular challenges faced by students and teachers to bring argumentation into the classroom. For instance, Kuhn (1993) has documented students' problems in distinguishing between theory and evidence and Lemke (1990) has critically examined teachers' issues with orchestrating classroom discourse. While some of this type of research focuses on written arguments (e.g., Bell 2000; Sandoval and Millwood 2005), much attention is also given to argumentation as part of classroom discourse (e.g., Kelly, Druker, and Chen 1998; Driver, Newton, and Osborne 2000).

12. The analyses of science conversations and arguments were conducted together with Jacqueline Wong (see Kafai and Wong 2008).

13. The recent NRC report (Bell et al. 2009) on learning science in informal settings highlights the importance for children's learning to become engaged in science outside of school.

14. For more detail on the implementation of WhyPox in an infectious disease curriculum unit for upper elementary students, please consult Neulight, Kafai, Kao, Foley, and Galas (2007). Sections from this article reprinted here with kind permission from Springer Science+Business Media.

15. We used Au and Romo's (1999) scenarios and four-point rubric to assess students' understanding of infectious disease. If students included a biological causal explanation (e.g., a person got sick because germs grew, reproduced, and attacked cells), their response was given a higher score than a response that included only a nonbiological cause (e.g., a person got sick because he was not wearing a coat).

16. See Quintero 2007.

17. See, e.g., Angela Calabrese Barton's work (e.g., Barton 2003).

18. For a fuller description of the priority of making good avatars and socializing, see chapter 4, as well as Kafai, Cook, and Fields 2010 and Feldon and Kafai 2008.

19. See Lofgren and Fefferman 2007.

20. In July 2007, virtual worlds made the cover of *Science* magazine (Bainbridge 2007), with William Bainbridge emphasizing the research potential of virtual worlds

for scientists conducting virtual laboratory experiments. Virtual worlds offer electronic environments for people to viably work and interact and thus allow for certain studies of economic and social behaviors that may be otherwise difficult to implement with human participants.

21. For more information on RiverCity's design and learning outcomes, see Ketelhut 2007.

22. For more information on Quest Atlantis's design and learning outcomes, see Barab, Pettyjohn, Gresalfi, Volk, and Solomou 2012.

7 Designing Connected Play

1. Twigsy 2007.

2. The paragraph quoted is just the ending of a three-page-long article on how to design face parts.

3. See also Bartle's (2003) book on designing virtual worlds.

4. See Bers 2011.

5. For instance, Shrier (2005) and Squire (2004) found that while players became adept at using and understanding rules of the games they played (including such games as Civilization III in a history class), the young people unquestioningly accepted the norms, ideologies, and means of representation in the games.

6. See Boellstorff 2008.

7. As of October 8, 2006.

8. Posting answers to the chat license test was hardly scandalous. After taking the test once, the Whyville site would tell citizens which answers were incorrect, what the correct answers were, and allow them to retake the test. Posting all of the answers up front simply gave a shortcut.

9. See Consalvo's (2007) book on cheating.

10. Additions to Whyville since this research was conducted intentionally set up value-relevant decisions that must be acted on by individual Whyvillians and/or the community at large. For example, the WhyPower virtual power plant requires the community to vote weekly on the kinds of energy sources (coal, natural gas, nuclear, hydroelectric, wind, or solar) to be allowed in Whyville the following week. Whyvillians assess community needs, evaluate economic efficiencies, but ultimately make a value-based vote on power policy. A curriculum has been developed to intentionally bring this discussion into formal classrooms.

11. Even though the designers of GameSite.net posted answers to the chat test, they strongly encouraged players to read things properly and take the time to understand

what the test was about. This supports Whyville's own policy of displaying correct answers to the test after a player takes the test so that they can learn from experience.

12. As of November 7, 2011, Minecraft had over 16 million registered users and over 4 million purchases (*source:* Wikipedia).

13. For more information on Scratch, see http://scratch.mit.edu and Resnick et al. 2009.

14. See Kafai, Fields, and Burke 2010.

15. See Fields and Enyedy forthcoming.

16. See Kafai, Peppler, and Chapman 2009.

8   Future Play

1. Bluwave was one of at least two avatars Zoe created in Whyville but the only one we knew and followed.

2. See the report by Grimes and Fields (2012).

3. There is a long tradition of studying play by notable researchers such as Opie and Opie (1985), Sutton Smith (1981), and many others.

4. See Thorne 1993.

5. In *Engineering Play*, Ito (2008) makes a compelling case for how the production of children's software embodies the "intertwining of different genres, social agendas and educational philosophies" (187).

6. In *Designing Digital Experiences for Positive Youth Development*, Marina Bers (2011) outlines three digital landscapes—from playpen to playground in early childhood years, from multimedia parks to virtual malls in elementary school years, and from wireless hangouts to a palace in time for high school years—for kids' and youth' personal development.

7. The recent FTC report "Mobile Apps for Kids: Disclosures Still Not Making the Grade" (Federal Trade Commission 2012) discusses how commercial companies collect data without consent.

8. For an overview, see the handbook on virtual worlds research by Boellstorff, Nardi, Pearce, and Taylor (2012).

9. For more detail, see the Research Notes.

10. Here we make reference to Geertz's (1973) notion of "thick" descriptions.

11. Grimes and Fields (2012) argued this in a recent report on children and networked media.

12. Ito et al. 2010.

13. Celia Pearce's (2011) work on migration in MMORPGs is one of the leading examples here.

14. Consider, e.g., the several commercial virtual worlds designed for children that have been studied by Rebecca Black (Black and Reich 2011) and Sara Grimes (Grimes 2008a,b; Grimes and Shade 2005).

15. Goodwin 2006.

16. For instance, many sites for children have much stronger chat filters than Whyville, so much so that some even promote incorrect grammar, for instance not allowing the word "come" (Black 2010; Black and Reich 2011). Instead, while Whyville does have a chat filter, it is not as strict as others and instead requires citizens to take a test that teaches protocols for safety and appropriate behavior, as well as reporting mechanisms for when people do violate norms.

17. Parts of this section drawn from Y. B. Kafai and K. A. Searle, "Safeguarding Play in Virtual Worlds: Designs and Perspectives on Tween Player Participation in Community Management," from *International Journal of Learning and Media*, fall 2010, vol. 2, no. 4, pp. 31–42, © 2011 Massachusetts Institute of Technology, by permission of The MIT Press.

18. See Consalvo 2007; Fields and Kafai 2010b; Stevens, Satwicz, and McCarthy 2008.

19. See Greenfield 2004.

20. While this may be seen as risky, the literature on sex education and older teens suggests that making practice decisions and receiving feedback from a more knowledgeable individual can be an important part of making the right decision when it really matters.

21. Grimes and Fields 2012.

22. Jenkins 1998/2005.

23. See Cassell and Cramer 2008.

24. Grimes 2010.

25. Some exceptions include the online games GirlSense and Barbie Girls, where the world is focused on dressing up.

26. See Seiter 2007 and Kellner 1995.

27. See Kafai and Fields 2009.

28. See, e.g., Prensky 2001.

Research Notes

1. See Boellstorff, Nardi, Pearce, and Taylor 2012.

2. See Kraut, Olson, Banaji, Bruckman, Cohen, and Couper 2004.

3. See Williams 2005.

4. See Yee 2008.

5. See Gee 2003 and Taylor 2006.

6. See Feldon and Kafai 2008.

7. The total number of consenting online participants includes students and members from the school classes and after-school clubs. For some analyses, such as the use of the epidemic simulators during Whypox outbreak, we excluded the group of students because we were interested in voluntary participation. For other analyses, we included only those participants who completed all answers in surveys.

8. See Kafai, Feldon, Fields, Giang, and Quintero 2007.

9. See Kafai and Giang 2008 and Neulight et al. 2007.

10. See Kafai and Fields 2012.

11. See Kafai 2008.

12. This analysis has all the features of traditional cluster analysis (e.g., k-means approach, model fit criteria based on log-likelihood distance, and Bayesian criteria).

13. See Leander 2008 and Leander, Phillips, and Taylor 2010.

14. Some researchers have used logfiles selectively over a short period of time, for instance two girls over a few days (Bruckman 2000) or a small group during a few class periods (Clarke and Dede 2007). Others have done extensive quantitative analysis of logfiles (e.g., Williams, Yee, and Caplan 2008) or analyses of social networks (Ducheneaut, Yee, Nickell, and Moore 2006) or combined multiple data sources (Feldon and Kafai 2008). Perhaps the most common qualitative use of logfiles is to collect and analyze chat (Nardi, Ly, and Harris 2007), but collection of chat has generally been limited to whatever place the researcher virtually inhabits at a given time.

15. See Fields and Kafai 2012; Kafai and Fields 2012; Kafai, Fields, and Searle 2010.

16. The field of data analytics of such massive data sets has been gaining considerable traction in recent years.

References

Aquagerl. 2002. More than outside. *Whyville Times*, December 5. http://j.whyville .net/smmk/whytimes/article?id=2139.

Artista. 2005. In a Latino's shoes. *Whyville Times*, July 13. http://www.whyville.net/ smmk/whytimes/article?id=5301.

Aschbacher, Pamela R. 2003. *Gender Differences in the Perception and Use of an Informal Science Learning Web Site: Final Project Report to the National Science Foundation*. Pasadena: California Institute of Technology.

Au, Terry Kit-Fong, and Laura F. Romo. 1996. Building a coherent conception of HIV transmission: A new approach to AIDS education. *Psychology of Learning and Motivation* 35:193–241.

Au, Terry Kit-Fong, and Laura F. Romo. 1999. Mechanical causality in children's folkbiology. In *Folkbiology*, ed. Douglas Medin and Scott Atran, 355–403. Cambridge, MA: MIT Press.

Bainbridge, William Sims. 2007. The scientific research potential of virtual worlds. *Science* 317 (5837):472–476.

Barab, Sasha, Patrick Pettyjohn, Melissa Gresalfi, Charlene Volk, and Maria Solomou. 2012. Game-based curriculum and transformational play: Designing to meaningfully positioning person, content, and context. *Computers and Education* 58 (1):518–533.

Barab, Sasha, Michael Thomas, Tyler Dodge, Robert Carteaux, and Hakan Tuzun. 2005. Making learning fun: Quest Atlantis, a game without guns. *Educational Technology Research and Development* 53 (1):86–107.

Bartle, Richard. 2003. *Designing Virtual Worlds*. New York: New Riders.

Barton, Angela Calabrese. 2003. *Teaching Science for Social Justice*. New York: Teachers College Press.

Bell, Philip. 2000. Scientific arguments as learning artifacts: Designing for learning from the Web with KIE. *International Journal of Science Education* 22 (8):797–817.

Bell, Philip, Bruce Lewenstein, Andrew W. Shouse, and Michael A. Feder, eds. 2009. *Learning Science in Informal Environments: People, Places, and Pursuits*. Washington, DC: National Academies Press.

Bergen, Doris, ed. 1998. *Play from Birth to Twelve: Contexts, Perspectives, and Meanings*. New York: Garland Publishing.

Berman, Joshua, and Amy S. Bruckman. 2001. The Turing game: Exploring identity in an online environment. *Convergence* 7 (3):83–102.

Bers, Marina Umaschi. 2011. *Designing Digital Experiences for Positive Youth Development*. New York: Oxford University Press.

Black, Rebecca. 2010. The language of *Webkinz*: Early childhood literacy in an online virtual world. *Digital Culture and Education* 2 (1):7–24.

Black, Rebecca, and Stephanie Reich. 2011. Affordances and constraints of scaffolded learning in a virtual world for young children. *International Journal of Game-Based Learning* 1 (2):52–64.

Bluegal7. 2002. It's the inside that counts. *Whyville Times*, Aug. 1. http://j.whyville .net/smmk/whytimes/article?id=1601.

Boellstorff, Tim. 2008. *Coming of Age in Second Life: An Anthropologist Explores the Virtually Human*. Princeton: Princeton University Press.

Boellstorff, Tom, Bonnie Nardi, Celia Pearce, and T. L. Taylor. 2012. *Ethnography and Virtual Worlds: A Handbook of Method*. Princeton: Princeton University Press.

boyd, danah. 2007. Why youth (heart) social network sites: The role of networked publics in teenage social life. In *Youth, Identity, and Digital Media*, ed. David Buckingham. The John D. and Catherine T. MacArthur Foundation Series on Digital Media and Learning. Cambridge, MA: MIT Press.

Bruckman, Amy. 2000. Situated support for learning: Storm's Weekend with Rachael. *Journal of the Learning Sciences* 9 (3):329–372.

Burnam, Bruce, and Yasmin Kafai. 2001. Computers and ethics: Children's moral reasoning about computer and internet uses. *Journal of Educational Computing Research* 25 (2):111–127.

Casc302. 2006. To date or not to date: That is the question. *Whyville Times*. http:// www.Whyville.net.

Cassell, Justine, and Meg Cramer. 2008. High tech or high risk: Moral panics about girls online. In *Digital Youth, Innovation, and the Unexpected*, ed. Tara McPherson, 53–76. Cambridge, MA: MIT Press.

Castronova, Edward. 2006. *Synthetic Worlds: The Business and Culture of Online Games*. Chicago: University of Chicago Press.

Ching, Cynthia Carter, and Yasmin B. Kafai. 2008. Peer pedagogy: Student collaboration and reflection in learning through design. *Teachers College Record* 110 (12):2601–2632.

Clarke, Jody, and Chris Dede. 2007. MUVEs as a powerful means to study situated learning. In *The Proceedings of CSCL 2007: Of Mice, Minds, and Society*, ed. C. Chinn, G. Erkins, and S. Puntambekar. Utrecht, Netherlands: International Society of the Learning Sciences.

Colella, Vanessa. 2000. Participatory simulations: Building collaborative understanding through immersive dynamic modeling. *Journal of the Learning Sciences* 9 (4):471–500.

Common Sense Media. 2011. Zero to eight: Children's media use in America. San Francisco: Common Sense Media Report. http://www.commonsensemedia.org/research/zero-eight-childrens-media-use-america.

Consalvo, Mia. 2007. *Cheating: Gaining Advantage in Video Games*. Cambridge, MA: MIT Press.

Cook, Daniel, and Susan Kaiser. 2004. Betwixt and between. *Journal of Consumer Culture* 4 (2):203–229.

Corsaro, William. 2005. *The Sociology of Childhood*, 2nd ed. London: Pine Forge Press.

Dede, Chris, Brian Nelson, Diane J. Ketelhut, J. Clarke, and Cassie Bowman. 2004. Design-based research strategies for studying situated learning in a multi-user virtual environment. In *Proceedings of the Sixth International Conference of the Learning Sciences*, ed. Yasmin B. Kafai, William Sandoval, Noel Enyedy, Althea Nixon, and Francisco Herrera. Mahwah, NJ: Erlbaum.

Deterding, Sebastian, Dan Dixon, Rilla Khaled, and Lennart Nacke. 2011. From game design elements to gamefulness: Defining "gamification." In *Proceedings of the 15th International Academic MindTrek Conference: Envisioning Future Media Environments (MindTrek '11)*. New York: ACM Press.

DiGsTeR02. 2005. Return of the WhyPox! *Whyville Times*, Feb. 6. http://j.whyville .net/smmk/whytimes/article?id=4928.

Driver, Rosalind, Paul Newton, and Jonathan Osborne. 2000. Establishing the norms of scientific argumentation in classrooms. *Science Education* 84 (3):287–312.

Ducheneaut, Nicolas, Nick Yee, Eric Nickell, and Robert Moore. 2006. Building an MMO with mass appeal: A look at gameplay in World of Warcraft. *Games and Culture* 1:281–317.

Ellison, Nicole, Charles Steinfield, and Cliff Lampe. 2007. The benefits of Facebook "friends": Exploring the relationship between college students' use of online social networks and social capital. *Journal of Computer-Mediated Communication* 12 (3):1143–1168.

Elkind, David. 1979. *All Grown Up and No Place to Go: Teenagers in Crisis*. Cambridge: Perseus Books.

EIEmAyeOh. 2011. Am I perfect yet? *Whyville Times*, July 31. http://j.whyville.net/smmk/whytimes/article?id=12271.

Engeström, Yrjö. 2008. From design experiments to formative interventions. In *Proceedings of the 8th International Conference of the Learning Sciences*, vol. 1, ed. V. Jonker, A. Lazonder, and C. Hoadley, 3–26. Utrecht, Netherlands: International Society of the Learning Sciences.

Epstein, Marina, and L. Monique Ward. 2008. Always use protection: Communication boys receive about sex from parents, peers, and the media. *Journal of Youth and Adolescence* 37 (2):113–126.

Erikson, Erik. 1968. *Identity: Youth and Crisis*. New York: Norton.

Expressing yourself through face parts. 2002. *Whyville Times*, Jan. 17. http://j.whyville.net/smmk/whytimes/article?id=938.

Feldon, David, and Joanna Gilmore. 2006. Patterns in children's online behavior and scientific problem-solving: A large-n microgenetic study. In *Avoiding Simplicity, Confronting Complexity: Advances in Studying and Designing (Computer-Based) Powerful Learning Environments*, ed. Geraldine Clarebout and Jan Elen, 117–125. Rotterdam: Sense Publishers.

Feldon, D., and Y. Kafai. 2008. Mixed methods for mixed reality: Understanding users' avatar activities in virtual worlds. *Educational Technology Research and Development* 56 (5–6):575–593.

Fields, Deborah A., and Noel Enyedy. 2013. Picking up the mantle of "expert": Assigned roles, assertion of identity, and peer recognition within a programming class. *Mind, Culture, and Activity: International Journal* 20 (2): 113–131.

Fields, Deborah A., and Yasmin B. Kafai. 2009. A connective ethnography of peer knowledge sharing and diffusion in a tween virtual world. *International Journal of Computer-Supported Collaborative Learning* 4 (1):47–68.

Fields, Deborah A., and Yasmin B. Kafai. 2010a. Knowing and throwing mudballs, hearts, pies, and flowers: A connective ethnography of gaming practices. *Games and Culture* 5 (1):88–115.

Fields, Deborah A., and Yasmin B. Kafai. 2010b. Stealing from grandma or generating knowledge? Contestations and effects of cheating in Whyville. *Games and Culture* 5 (1):64–87.

Fields, Deborah A., and Yasmin B. Kafai. 2012. Navigating life as an avatar: The shifting identities-in-practice of a girl player in a tween virtual world. In *Constructing Identity in a Digital World*, ed. Cynthia Carter Ching and Brian J. Foley, 222–250. Cambridge: Cambridge University Press.

Flanagan, Mary, and Helen Nussbaum. 2008. Value in games. In *Beyond Barbie and Mortal Kombat*, ed. Yasmin Kafai, Carrie Heeter, Jill Denner, and Jennifer Sun. Cambridge, MA: MIT Press.

Federal Trade Commission. 2012. *Mobile Apps for Kids: Disclosures Still Not Making the Grade*. Washington, DC.

Fromberg, Doris P., and Doris Bergen, eds. 2006. *Play from Birth to Twelve: Contexts, Perspectives, and Meanings*. New York: Garland Publishing.

Garvey, Catherine. 1984. *Children's Talk*. Cambridge, MA: Harvard University Press.

Gee, James Paul. 1999. *An Introduction to Discourse Analysis: Theory and Method*. London: Routledge.

Gee, James Paul. 2000–2001. Identity as an analytic lens for research in education. *Review of Research in Education* 25: 99–125.

Gee, James Paul. 2003. *What Video Games Have to Teach Us about Learning and Literacy*. New York: Palgrave Macmillan.

Gee, James Paul. 2004. *Situated Language and Learning: A Critique of Traditional Schooling*. New York: Routledge.

Geertz, Clifford. 1973. Thick description: Toward an interpretive theory of culture. In *The Interpretation of Cultures*, 3–30. New York: Basic Books.

Giang, Michael T., Yasmin B. Kafai, Deborah A. Fields, and Kristin A. Searle. 2012. Social interactions in virtual worlds: Patterns and participation of tween relationship play. In *Computer Games and New Media Cultures: A Handbook on the State and Perspectives of Digital Games Studies*, ed. Johannes Fromme and Alexander Unger, 543–556. New York: Springer.

Glaser, Barney, and Anselm Strauss. 1967. *The Discovery of Grounded Theory: Strategies for Qualitative Research*. Chicago: Aldine.

GoodPlay Project, The. 2011. Our space: Being a responsible citizen of the digital world. Harvard University. http://dmlcentral.net/sites/dmlcentral/files/resource _files/Our_Space_full_casebook_compressed.pdf.

Goodwin, Marjorie Harness. 2006. *Hidden Lives of Girls: Games of Stance, Status, and Exclusion*. Oxford: Blackwell.

Goodwin, Marjorie Harness. 2002. Exclusion in girls' peer groups: Ethnographic analysis of language practices on the playground. *Human Development* 45 (6):392–415.

Goodwin, Marjorie Harness. 1985. The serious side of jump rope: Conversational practices and social organization in the frame of play. *Journal of American Folklore* 98 (389):315–330.

Granovetter, Mark S. 1973. The strength of weak ties. *American Journal of Sociology* 78:1360–1380.

Greenfield, Patricia M. 2004. Developmental considerations for determining appropriate internet use guidelines for children and adolescents. *Journal of Applied Developmental Psychology* 25:751–762.

Grimes, Sara M. 2008. Kids' ad play: Regulating children's advergames in the converging media context. *International Journal of Communications Law and Policy* 8 (12): 162–178.

Grimes, Sara M. 2008b. The exploitation of children's affective labour in corporately owned virtual worlds. Paper presented at Joint Annual Meetings of Law and Society Association and Canadian Law and Society Association, Montreal, Quebec.

Grimes, Sara M. 2010. The digital child at play: How technological, political, and commercial rule systems shape children's play in virtual Worlds. PhD diss., Simon Fraser University.

Grimes, Sara M., and Deborah A. Fields. 2012. *Kids Online: A New Research Agenda for Understanding Social Networking Forums*. New York: Joan Ganz Cooney Center. Available at http://www.joanganzcooneycenter.org/reports-38.html.

Grimes, Sara M., and Leslie Shade. 2005. Neopian economics of play: Children's cyberpets and online communities as immersive advertising in Neopets.com. *International Journal of Media and Cultural Politics* 1 (2):181–198.

GrriesYEA. 2003. Cheating the system? *Whyville Times*, Feb. 28. http://j.whyville .net/smmk/whytimes/article?id=2494.

Hargittai, Eszter, and Gina Walejko. 2008. The participation divide: Content creation and sharing in the digital age. *Information Communication and Society* 11 (2):239–256.

Holland, Dorothy, William Lachicotte, Jr., Debra Skinner, and Carole Cain. 1998. *Identity and Agency in Cultural Worlds*. Cambridge, MA: Harvard University Press.

Holiday50. 2008. I hate you for Whydating. *Whyville Times*, April 13. Accessed November 2, 2008. http://j.whyville.net/smmk/whytimes/article?id=8654.

Hutchins, Edwin. 1995. *Cognition in the Wild*. Cambridge, MA: MIT Press.

Ickamcoy. 2003. Cheat sites! *Whyville Times*, Sept. 25. http://j.whyville.net/smmk/whytimes/article?id=3247.

Ito, M. 2010. *Engineering Play*. Cambridge, MA: MIT Press.

Ito, Mimi, and Heather Horst. 2006. Neopoints and neo economies: Emergent regimes of value in kids peer-to-peer networks. American Anthropological Association Meetings. http://www.itofisher.com/mito/itohorst.neopets.pdf.

Ito, Mizuko. 2008. *Engineering Play: A Cultural History of Children's Software*. Cambridge, MA: MIT Press.

Ito, Mizuko, Heather Horst, Matteo Bittanti, danah boyd, et al. 2010. *Hanging Out, Messing Around, Geeking Out: Living and Learning with New Media*. Cambridge, MA: MIT Press.

James, Carrie, Katie Davis, Andrea Flores, John Francis, Linsday Pettingill, Margaret Rundle, and Howard Gardner. 2009. *Young People, Ethics, and the New Digital Media*. Cambridge, MA: MIT Press.

JasmineK. 2004. Dating service in Whyville? *Whyville Times*, Feb. 6. http://j.whyville.net/smmk/whytimes/article?id=3697.

Jenkins, Henry. 1998/2005. Complete freedom of movement: Video games as gendered play spaces. In *The Game Design Reader*, ed. Katie Salen and Eric Zimmerman, 330–363. Cambridge, MA: MIT Press.

Jenkins, Henry, Katie Clinton, Ravi Purushotma, Alice J. Robinson, and Margaret Weigel. 2006. *Confronting the Challenges of Participatory Culture: Media Education for the 21st Century*. Chicago, IL: The John D. and Catherine T. MacArthur Foundation.

Kafai, Yasmin B. 2008. Gender play in a tween gaming club. In *Beyond Barbie and Mortal Kombat: New Perspectives on Gender and Gaming*, ed. Yasmin Kafai, Carrie Heeter, Jill Denner, and Jennifer Sun, 111–124. Cambridge, MA: MIT Press.

Kafai, Yasmin B., Melissa S. Cook, and Deborah A. Fields. 2010. "Blacks deserve bodies too!" Design and discussion about diversity and race in a tween virtual world. *Games and Culture* 5 (1):43–63.

Kafai, Yasmin B., and Deborah A. Fields. Connecting play: Understanding multimodal participation in virtual worlds. In *Proceedings of the 14th ACM International Conference on Multimodal Interaction*, 265–272. Santa Monica, CA: ACM.

Kafai, Yasmin B., and Deborah A. Fields. 2009. Cheating in virtual worlds: Transgressive designs for learning. *Horizon* 17 (1):12–20.

Kafai, Yasmin B., and Deborah A. Fields. 2012. Connecting play: Understanding multimodal participation in virtual worlds. In *Proceedings of the 14th International Conference on Multimodal Interaction*, 265–272. Santa Monica, CA: ACM.

Kafai, Yasmin B., Deborah A. Fields, and William Quinn Burke. 2010. Entering the clubhouse: Case studies of young programmers joining the scratch community. *Journal of Organizational and End User Computing* 22 (2):21–35.

Kafai, Yasmin B., Deborah A. Fields, and Melissa S. Cook. 2010. Your second selves: Player-designed avatars. *Games and Culture* 5 (1):23–42.

Kafai, Yasmin B., Deborah A. Fields, and Kristin A. Searle. 2010. Multi-modal investigations of relationship play in virtual worlds. *International Journal of Gaming and Computer-Mediated Simulations* 2 (1):40–48.

Kafai, Yasmin B., and Michael T. Giang. 2008. Virtual playgrounds: Children's multi-user virtual environments for playing and learning with science. In *Children's Learning in a Digital World*, ed. Teena Willoughby and Eileen Woo, 196–217. Oxford: Blackwell.

Kafai, Yasmin B., Althea Scott Nixon, and Bruce Burnam. 2007. Digital dilemmas: How elementary preservice teachers reason about students' appropriate computer and internet use. *Journal of Technology and Teacher Education* 15 (3):409–424.

Kafai, Yasmin B., Kylie Peppler, and Robin Chapman, eds. 2009. *The Computer Clubhouse: Constructionism and Creativity in the Inner City*. New York: Teachers College Press.

Kafai, Yasmin B., Maria Quintero, and David Feldon. 2010. Investigating the "why" in Whypox: Explorations of a virtual epidemic. *Games and Culture* 5 (1):116–135.

Kafai, Yasmin B., and Kristin A. Searle. 2011. Safeguarding play in virtual worlds: Designs and perspectives on tween player participation in community management. *International Journal of Learning and Media* 2:1–14.

Kafai, Yasmin B., and Jacqueline Wong. 2008. Real arguments about a virtual epidemic: Conversations and contestations in a tween gaming club. In *Proceedings of the 8th International conference on International Conference for the Learning Sciences*, vol. 1, pp. 414–421. Utrecht, Netherlands: International Society of the Learning Sciences.

Kalish, Charles W. 1999. What young children's understanding of contamination and contagion tells us about their concepts of illness. In *Children's Understanding of Biology and Health*, ed. Michael Siegal and Candida Peterson, 99–130. Cambridge: Cambridge University Press.

KamuiX. 2002. The two most annoying questions. *Whyville Times*, Dec. 5. http://j .whyville.net/smmk/whytimes/article?id=2145.

Kellner, Douglas. 1995. *Media Culture: Cultural Studies, Identity and Politics between the Modern and the Postmodern*. London: Taylor & Francis.

Kelly, Gregory J., Stephen Druker, and Catherine Chen. 1998. Students' reasoning about electricity: Combining performance assessments with argumentation analysis. *International Journal of Science Education* 20 (7):849–871.

Kemario. 2005. Labelling in Whyville. *Whyville Times*, May 22. http://h.whyville .net/smmk/whytimes/article?id=5283.

Ketelhut, Diane Jass. 2007. The impact of student self-efficacy on scientific inquiry skills: An exploratory investigation in river city, a multi-user virtual environment. *Journal of Science Education and Technology* 16 (1):99–111.

Kolko, Beth. 1998. Bodies in place: Real politics, real pedagogy, and virtual space. In *High Wired: On the Design, Use, and Theory of Educational MOOs*, ed. Cynthia Haynes and Jan Rune Holmvik, 253–265. Ann Arbor: University of Michigan Press.

Kraut, Robert, Judith Olson, Mahzarin Banaji, Amy Bruckman, Jeffrey Cohen, and Mick Couper. 2004. Psychological research online: Opportunities and challenges. *American Psychologist* 59:105–117.

Kroger, Jane. 2000. *Identity Development: Adolescence through Adulthood.* Thousand Oaks: Sage.

Kuhn, Deanna. 1993. Science as argument: Implications for teaching and learning scientific thinking. *Science Education* 77 (3):319–337.

Kuhn, D., and E. Phelps. 1982. The development of problem-solving strategies. In *Advances in Child Development and Behavior,* ed. Hayne W. Reese, 2–44. New York: Academic Press.

Kyratzis, Amy. 2004. Talk and interaction among children and the co-construction of peer groups and peer culture. *Annual Review of Anthropology* 33:625–649.

Lam, Wan Shun Eva. 2000. Second language literacy and the design of the self: A case study of a teenager writing on the Internet. *TESOL Quarterly* 34:457–483.

Lam, Wan Shun Eva. 2009. Multiliteracies on instant messaging in negotiating local, translocal, and transnational affiliations: A case of an adolescent immigrant. *Reading Research Quarterly* 44 (4):377–397.

Larson, Reed W. 2000. Towards a psychology of positive youth development. *American Psychologist* 55:170–183.

Lave, Jean, and Etienne Wenger. 1991. *Situated Learning and Legitimate Peripheral Participation.* Cambridge: Cambridge University Press.

Leander, Kevin. 2008. Toward a connective ethnography of online/offline literacy networks. In *Handbook of Research on New Literacies,* ed. D. Leu, J. Cairo, Michelle Knobel, and Colin Lankshear, 33–65. Mahwah, NJ: Erlbaum.

Leander, Kevin, and Amy Frank. 2006. The aesthetic production and distribution of image/subjects among online youth. *E-learning* 3 (2): 185–206.

Leander, Kevin M., Nathan C. Phillips, and Katherine Headrick Taylor. 2010. The changing social spaces of learning: Mapping new mobilities. *Review of Research in Education* 34:329–394.

Lee, Joey J., and Christopher M. Hoadley. 2006. Ugly in a world where you can choose to be beautiful: Teaching and learning about diversity via virtual worlds. In *Proceedings of the 7th International Conference on Learning Sciences,* pp. 383–389. Utrecht, Netherlands: International Society of the Learning Sciences.

Lee, Joey, and Christopher Hoadley. 2007. Leveraging identity to make learning fun: Possible selves and experiential learning in massively multiplayer online games (MMOGs). *Innovate* 3 (6).

Lemke, Jay L. 1990. *Talking Science: Language, Learning, and Values*, vol. 1. New York: Ablex.

Lenhart, Amanda, Kristin Purcell, Aaron Smith, and Kathryn Zickuhr. 2010. *Social Media and Mobile Internet Use among Teens and Young Adults*. Pew Internet & American Life Project, an initiative of the Pew Research Center.

Lenhart, Amanda, and Mary Madden. 2007. Social networking websites and teens: An overview. Pew Internet & American Life Project. http://www.pewinternet.org/pdfs/PIP_SNS_Data_Memo_Jan_2007.pdf.

Lethal guinea pig kills virtual people. 2000. BBC News. http://news.bbc.co.uk/2/hi/science/nature/746700.stm.

Lilly2000. 2000. Announcements and Advertisements. *Whyville Times*, Nov. 20. http://j.whyville.net/smmk/whytimes/article?id=419

Liss22. 2002. Racism, clothes, and city workers. *Whyville Times*, Sept. 19. http://j.whyville.net/smmk/whytimes/article?id=1835.

Liss22, and Piker. 2002. Behind the veil. *Whyville Times*, July 18. http://j.whyville.net/smmk/whytimes/article?id=1533.

Livingstone, Sonia, Leslie Haddon, Anke Gorzig, and Kjartan Olafsson. 2011. *EU Kids Online II: Final Report*. London: EC Safer Internet Program.

Lloyd, Barbara, and Gerard Duveen. 1992. *Gender Identities and Education: The Impact of Starting School*. New York: St. Martin's Press.

Lofgren, Eric T., and Nina H. Fefferman. 2007. The untapped potential of virtual game worlds to shed light on real world epidemics. *Lancet Infectious Diseases* 7 (9):625–629.

LukeG. 2002. A kinder heart. *Whyville Times*, Aug. 15. http://j.whyville.net/smmk/whytimes/article?id=1643.

MacCabe, Donald L., Linda Klebe Trevino, and Kenneth D. Butterfield. 2001. Cheating in academic institutions: A decade of research. *Ethics and Behavior* 11 (3):219–232.

Marsh, Jackie. 2010. Young children's play in online virtual worlds. *Journal of Early Childhood Research* 8 (1):23–39.

Mikay37. 2003. Be careful! *Whyville Times*, Feb. 15. http://j.whyville.net/smmk/whytimes/article?id=2392.

Nakamura, Lisa. 2001. *Cybertypes: Race, Ethnicity, and Identity on the Internet*. New York: Routledge.

Nardi, Bonnie A., Stella Ly, and Justin Harris. 2007. Learning conversation in World of Warcraft. In *Proceedings of the 40th Hawaii International Conference on*

System Sciences. http://origin-www.computer.org/csdl/proceedings/hicss/2007/2755/ 00/27550079a.pdf.

National Research Council. 2000. *Being Fluent in Information Technology*. Washington, DC: National Academy Press.

National Research Council. 2009. *Learning Science in Informal Environments: People, Places, and Pursuits*. Washington, DC: The National Academies Press.

Neulight, Nina, Yasmin B. Kafai, Linda Kao, Brian Foley, and Cathleen Galas. 2007. Children's learning about infectious disease through participation in a virtual epidemic. *Journal of Science Education and Technology* 16 (1):47–58.

Norman, Donald. 2005. In defense of cheating. *Ubiquity* 6 (11). doi: 10.1145/ 1066346.1066347.

Obeidallah, Dawn, Patricia Turner, Ronald J. Iannotti, Robert W. O'Brien, Denise Haynie, and Daniel Galper. 1993. Investigating children's knowledge and understanding of AIDS. *Journal of School Health* 63 (3):125–129.

Opie, Iona, and Peter Opie. 1969. *Children's Games in Street and Playground*. New York: Oxford University Press.

Opie, Iona, and Peter Opie. 1985. *The Singing Game*. Oxford: Oxford University Press.

oSTEPHo. 2002. Scamming Grandma scums! *Whyville Times*, Nov. 14. http://j .whyville.net/smmk/whytimes/article?id=2069.

Pearce, Celia. 2011. *Communities of Play*. Cambridge, MA: MIT Press.

Phinney, Jean S. 1989. Stages of ethnic identity development in minority group adolescents. *Journal of Early Adolescence* 9:34–49.

PixiBritt. 2005. Biddigurl's Kelcie army. *Whyville Times*, May 22. http://j.whyville .net/smmk/whytimes/article?id=5281.

Prejudice: Not only race. 2003. *Whyville Times*, Aug. 1. http://j.whyville.net/smmk/ whytimes/article?id=3045.

Prensky, Marc. 2001. Digital natives, digital immigrants. *Horizon* 9 (5):1–6.

Piaget, Jean. 1951. *Plays, Dreams, and Imitation in Childhood*. New York: Norton.

Punkst3r. 2000. Announcements and Advertisements: Church. *Whyville Times*, Nov. 2. http://j.whyville.net/smmk/whytimes/article?id=419.

Quintero, Maria. 2007. The "why" in Whypox: Teens' investigations of a virtual epidemic in an online world. Unpublished master's thesis, University of California, Los Angeles, Los Angeles.

RachelJay. 2002. Scamming Grandma! *Whyville Times*, Aug. 22. http://j.whyville .net/smmk/whytimes/article?id=1670.

Resnick, Mitchel, John Maloney, Andres Monroy Hernández, Natalie Rusk, Evelyn Eastmond, Karen Brennan, Amon D. Millner, et al. 2009. Scratch: Programming for everyone. *Communications of the ACM* 52 (11):60–67.

Rideout, Victoria J., Ulla G. Foehr, and Donald F. Roberts. 2010. Generation M^2: Media in the lives of 8–18-year-olds. Kaiser Family Foundation. http://www.kff.org/entmedia/upload/8010.pdf.

Salen, Katie, and Eric Zimmerman. 2004. *Rules of Play: Game Design Fundamentals.* Cambridge, MA: MIT Press.

Samgirl. 2003. Black like me. *Whyville Times*, July 13. http://j.whyville.net/smmk/whytimes/article?id=3019.

Sandoval, William A., and Kelli A. Millwood. 2005. The quality of students' use of evidence in written scientific explanations. *Cognition and Instruction* 23 (1):23–55.

Schauble, Leona. 1990. Belief revision in children: The role of prior knowledge and strategies for generating evidence. *Journal of Experimental Child Psychology* 32:102–119.

Schauble, Leona, Leopold E. Klopfer, and Kalyani Raghavan. 1991. Students transition from an engineering model to a science model of experimentation. *Journal of Research in Science Teaching* 28:859–882.

Searle, Kristin A., and Yasmin B. Kafai. Forthcoming. Beyond freedom of movement: Boys play in a tween virtual world. *Games and Culture.*

Seiter, Ellen. 2007. *The Internet Playground.* New York: Peter Lang.

Shavelson, Richard J., Gail P. Baxter, and Xiaohong Gao. 1993. Sampling variability of performance assessments. *Journal of Educational Measurement* 30 (3):215–232.

Shrier, Karen. 2005. Revolutionizing history education: Using augmented reality games to teach history. Master's thesis, Massachusetts Institute of Technology, Cambridge, Massachusetts.

Siegal, Michael. 1988. Children's understanding of contagion and contamination as causes of illness. *Child Development* 59 (4–6):1353–1359.

Siegal, Michael, and Candida C. Peterson. 1999. Becoming mindful of biology and health: An introduction. In *Children's Understanding of Biology and Health*, ed. Michael Siegal and Candida C. Peterson, 1–22. Cambridge: Cambridge University Press.

Sigelman, Carol K., Antonio L. Estrada, Eileen B. Derenowski, and Teresa E. Woods. 1996. Intuitive theories of human immunodeficiency virus transmission: Their development and implications. *Journal of Pediatric Psychology* 21 (4):555–572.

Singer, Jerome, and Dorothy Singer. 1992. *The House of Make Believe.* Cambridge, MA: Harvard University Press.

Singer, Dorothy, and Jerome Singer. 2005. *Imagination and Play in the Electronic Age*. Cambridge, MA: Harvard University Press.

Skop, Emily, and Paul C. Adams. 2009. Creating and inhabiting virtual places: Indian immigrants in cyberspace. *National Identities* 11 (2):127–147.

Šmahel, David, and Kaveri Subrahmanyam. 2007. Any girls want to chat press 911: Partner selection in monitored and unmonitored teen chat rooms. *Cyberpsychology and Behavior* 10:346–353.

Solis, Brian. 2010. *Engage: The Complete Guide for Brands and Businesses to Build, Cultivate, and Measure Success in the New Web*. Hoboken: John Wiley & Sons.

Squire, Kurt. 2004. Replaying history: Learning world history through playing Civilization III. PhD diss., Indiana University.

Squire, Kurt, and Sasha A. Barab. 2004. Replaying history: Engaging urban underserved students in learning world history through computer simulation games. In *Proceedings of the Sixth International Conference of the Learning Sciences*, ed. Yasmin B. Kafai, William Sandoval, Noel Enyedy, Althea Nixon, and Francisco Herrera. Mahwah, NJ: Erlbaum.

Steinfield, Charles, Nicole B. Ellison, and Cliffe Lampe. 2008. Social capital, self-esteem, and use of online social network sites: A longitudinal analysis. *Journal of Applied Developmental Psychology* 29:434–445.

Steinkuehler, Constance A. 2006. Massively multiplayer online video gaming as participation in a discourse. *Mind, Culture, and Activity* 13 (1):38–52.

Steinkuehler, Constance, and Sean Duncan. 2009. Scientific habits of mind in virtual worlds. *Journal of Science Education and Technology* 17:530–543.

Stevens, Reed, Tom Satwicz, and Laurie McCarthy. 2008. Game, in-room, in-world: Reconnecting video game play to the rest of kids' lives. In *The Ecology of Games: Connecting Youth, Games, and Learning*, ed. Katie Salen, 41–66. Cambridge, MA: MIT Press.

Subrahmanyam, Kaveri, Patricia Greenfield, and Brendesha Tynes. 2004. Constructing sexuality and identity in an internet teen chatroom. *Journal of Applied Developmental Psychology* 25: 651–666.

Subrahmanyam, Kaveri, Stephanie M. Reich, Natalia Waechter, and Guadalupe Espinoza. 2008. Online and offline social networks: Use of social networking sites by emerging adults. *Journal of Applied Developmental Psychology* 29:420–433.

Subrahmanyam, Kaveri, David Šmahel, and Patricia M. Greenfield. 2006. Connecting developmental processes to the Internet: Identity presentation and sexual exploration in online teen chatrooms. *Developmental Psychology* 42:1–12.

Sulake. 2012. Habbo Hotel: Where else? http://www.sulake.com/habbo/?navi=2.

Sutton Smith, Brian. 1981. *A History of Children's Play*. Philadelphia, PA: University of Pennsylvania Press.

Sweden. 2005. A newbie day to remember. *Whyville Times*, Jan. 2. http://j.whyville .net/smmk/whytimes/article?id=4827.

Tami324. 2000. Blacks deserve bodies too! *Whyville Times*, June 1. http://j.whyville .net/smmk/whytimes/article?id=193.

Taylor, T. L. 1999. Life in virtual worlds: Plural existence, multimodalities, and other online research challenges. *American Behavioral Scientist* 43:436–449.

Taylor, T. L. 2006. *Play between Worlds*. Cambridge, MA: MIT Press.

Theboy2. 2005. Why, why, why pox? *Whyville Times*, Feb. 13. http://j.whyville.net/ smmk/whytimes/article?id=4956.

Thorne, Barrie. 1993. *Gender Play: Boys and Girls in School*. New Brunswick: Rutgers University Press.

Tike. 2003. Action, reaction, and a change in face. *Whyville Times*, Jan. 24. http://j .whyville.net/smmk/whytimes/article?id=2336.

Turkle, Sherry. 1984. *The Second Self: Computer and the Human Spirit*. New York: Simon & Schuster.

Turkle, Sherry. 1995. *Life on the Screen: Identity in the Age of the Internet*. New York: Simon & Schuster.

Turkle, Sherry. 2011. *Alone Together: Why We Expect More from Technology and Less from Each Other*. New York: Basic Books.

Twigsy. 2002. Scam busters. *Whyville Times*, May 30. http://j.whyville.net/smmk/ whytimes/article?id=1359.

Twigsy. 2007. So you want to be a designer? *Whyville Times*, July 20. http://j .whyville.net/smmk/whytimes/article?id=7199.

Tynes, Brendesha, Lindsay Reynolds, and Patricia M. Greenfield. 2004. Adolescence, race, and ethnicity on the Internet: A comparison of discourse in monitored vs. unmonitored chat rooms. *Journal of Applied Developmental Psychology* 25 (6):667–684.

Tynes, Brendesha M. 2007a. Internet safety gone wild? Sacrificing the educational and psychosocial benefits of online social environments. *Journal of Adolescent Research* 22 (6):575–584.

Tynes, Brendesha M. 2007b. Role taking in online "classrooms": What adolescents are learning about race and ethnicity. *Developmental Psychology* 43 (6):1312–1320.

Tynes, Brendesha M., Elizabeth L. García, Michael T. Giang, and Nicole Coleman. 2010. The racial landscape of social network sites: Forging identity, community, and civic engagement. *I/S: A Journal of Law and Policy for the Information Society* 7:1–30.

Ünlüsoy, Asli, and Marianne de Haan. 2011. Youth networks: Ethno-cultural diversity and informal learning relations online. Poster presented at ISCAR, Rome, Italy, September 2011. http://www.uu.nl/wiredup/pdf/ISCAR%20POSTER%20Fleur%20 Prinsen.pdf.

Walkerdine, Valerie. 2007. Video games and childhood masculinity. In *Children, Gender, Video Games: Towards a Relational Approach to Multimedia*, 30–47. New York: Palgrave Macmillan.

Wilensky, Uri, and Walter Stroup. 1999. Learning through participatory simulations: Network-based design for systems learning in classrooms. In *Proceedings of the 1999 Conference on Computer-Supported Collaborative Learning*, 80. Utrecht, Netherlands: International Society of the Learning Sciences.

Wilgoren, Jodi. 2002. School cheating scandal tests a town's values. *New York Times*, Feb. 14, A1.

Williams, Dmitri. 2005. Bridging the methodological divide in game research. *Simulation and Gaming* 36 (4):1–17.

Williams, Dmitri, Nick Yee, and Scott Caplan. 2008. Who plays, how much, and why? A behavioral player census of virtual world. *Journal of Computer-Mediated Communication* 13:993–1018.

Vygotsky, L. S. 1978. *Mind in Society: The Development of Higher Psychological Processes.* Cambridge, MA: Harvard University Press.

XKaileeX. 2003. Anti-virtual dating. *Whyville Times*, May 16. http://j.whyville.net/ smmk/whytimes/article?id=2779.

xXOscarXx. 2003. A lookist world. *Whyville Times*, Nov. 27. http://j.whyville.net/ smmk/whytimes/article?id=3445.

Yee, Nick. 2008. Maps of digital desires: Exploring the topography of gender and play in online games. In *Beyond Barbie and Mortal Kombat*, ed. Yasmin Kafai, Carrie Heeter, Jill Denner, and Jennifer Sun, 83–96. Cambridge, MA: MIT Press.

Yee, Nick. 2006. The demographics, motivations, and derived experiences of users of massively-multiuser online graphical environments. *PRESENCE: Teleoperators and Virtual Environments* 15: 309–329.

Index

Note: Page numbers in italic type indicate figures or tables.